Praise for Macrina Wiederkehr's *The Song of the Seed*

"Macrina gently guides the reader into the rhythm of a monastic retreat—to be quiet and to ponder the deep gospel truths that can be found beneath the surface turmoil of modern life. In doing so, she reveals the imagination of a poet and the heart of a vibrant believer. Everyone can benefit, while being delighted, by her wisdom."
> —Demetrius Dumm, O.S.B., author of *Flowers in the Desert: A Spirituality of the Bible*

"With lyrical simplicity and poetic grace, Macrina Wiederkehr leads the reader into *lectio divina,* and through the responses of bending, mending, and tending to the spirit within. Making this retreat under her guidance, I found myself nourished and newly aware of the songs in my own soul and the gifts of my world."
> —Maria Harris, author of *Jubilee Time: Celebrating Women, Spirit and the Advent of Age*

"*The Song of the Seed* is a grace-filled and intimate weaving of gospel and life stories. Wiederkehr's writing style invites and enfolds the reader in a sense of being cherished in God."
> —Norvene Vest, author of *No Moment Too Small*

"In this wise book we learn that it's not always necessary to leave home in order to find deep spiritual renewal. Through this 'at-home retreat' Macrina Wiederkehr guides us to recover the longings of our hearts for the Divine in the most difficult place of all—the press and strain of daily life. In her illuminating way, she leads us to sing the sacred song of our life right where we are."
> —Sue Monk Kidd, author of *Circle of Trees*

The Song of the Seed

Other books by Macrina Wiederkehr, O.S.B.

Seasons of Your Heart

A Tree Full of Angels

The Song
of the Seed

A Monastic Way of Tending the Soul

Macrina Wiederkehr, O.S.B.

HarperSanFrancisco
An Imprint of HarperCollins*Publishers*

Grateful acknowledgment is made to the following for permission to reprint previously published material:

Alfred A. Knopf, Inc., and the Wallace Literary Agency, Inc., for lines from *Stone, Paper, Knife* by Marge Piercy. Copyright © 1983 by Marge Piercy. Reprinted by permission.

Ave Maria Press for an excerpt from *May I Have This Dance* by Joyce Rupp. Copyright © 1992 by Ave Maria Press, Notre Dame, IN 46556. All rights reserved. Used by permission of the publisher.

Scribner, a division of Simon & Schuster, Inc., and Macmillan Publishers Ltd. for an excerpt from *Gitanjali* by Rabindranath Tagore (New York: Collier Books, 1971).

Threshold Books for lines from *Quatrains of Rumi: Unseen Rain,* translated by John Moyne and Coleman Barks. Used by permission of Threshold Books, RD 4 Box 600, Putney, VT 05346.

Bible quotations, unless otherwise noted, are from the New Revised Standard Version of the Bible, copyright © 1989 by the Division of Christian Education of the National Council of Churches of Christ in the U.S.A. Used by permission.

FIRST EDITION

Library of Congress Cataloging-in-Publication Data:
Wiederkehr, Macrina.
The song of the seed : a monastic way of tending the soul /
Macrina Wiederkehr.
p.   cm.
ISBN 0–06–069552–8 (cloth)—ISBN 0–06–069554–4 (pbk.)
1. Retreats.   2. Meditations.   3. Prayer.   4. Spiritual life—Catholic
Church.   I. Title.
BX2375.W54   1995   95-9271
269'.6—dc20   CIP

95 96 97 98 99 ❖ RRD(H) 10 9 8 7 6 5 4 3 2 1

For my sisters in community
with whom I live the Word each day.

And for all the women
who were ever a part of
St. Scholastica Monastery,
Fort Smith, Arkansas.

May we meet in God's circle of love
cherished, forgiven, and healed.

For when all things
were in quiet silence
and the night
was in the midst of her course
your almighty Word
leapt down from heaven
from your royal throne.

Wisdom 18:14–15, Douay

Contents

Part II Mending: The Feast

Part III Tending: The Gift

Acknowledgments

My grateful appreciation goes to the women and men who, because of their steadfast search for the sacred in their lives, have inspired me to write this book. I am especially grateful for my readers and the participants in my retreats who have opened up the doors of their souls to me, thus enriching my life.

A sincere thank you to those who have had a unique part in the shaping of this book: Kandace Hawkinson, my editor, for her gracious assistance and extremely helpful suggestions; and Rachel Dietz, who used many of my Scripture themes for her prayer and shared much of her journaling with me.

Special thanks to those colleagues who read my manuscript in whole or in part and offered valuable advice and encouragement: Consuella Bauer, Norbert Hoelting, Judy Hoelzeman, Joyce Rupp, and Jan Ord.

Thank you to Ron Meyers, who so willingly rescues me from my foibles with the computer.

Finally, I owe much to my community support group: Audrey, Gertie, Rosalie, and Stephanie, who pull me out of my office and on toward greater things. And to Kay, who works behind the scenes.

Introduction

A Word of power leapt from the heavens. It was the same Word that was *in the beginning* with God. This Word became God's enfleshed presence on the earth. It will be your guide during this retreat.

There is a renewed interest in retreats today. Perhaps it is because many of us lead such busy lives. There is an intense desire in people's hearts to connect with the spiritual self. We are looking for ways to nourish the soul.

Sometimes all that we yearn for—beauty, courage, love, hope, faith—lies hidden. God seems to be absent from our lives. We are unable to truly see the people with whom we live. The goodness and worth of our own lives elude us. At times like this we may feel called to take a step back and look at the mystery of life anew. That's what the word *retreat* means—to go back.

Can you recall a time when you came upon something of exquisite beauty? It may have been the silhouette of a tree in the sunset, the artistic design of a spider web in the morning sunlight, or a mother duck with her ducklings. Quite naturally you found yourself stepping back a little so that you could have a better look. You were too close to the object of beauty. Your step backward enabled you to see it all from another perspective, and so to see it more truly. Sometimes we miss things because we are standing too close to them.

A retreat is a time to step back and take a new look at our lives. It is not so much a time to learn new things as to remember and feel again some of the things we have forgotten. It is a time to be lovingly attentive to the needs of the soul.

What simple truths and values in our lives have been lost because of the busyness of our days? Has our intimacy with God and others suffered because we have too readily embraced the distractions and noise surrounding us? Has the simplicity of earlier days been crowded out by our drive to possess or control? What sacred stories from the past are buried in our souls? What are we missing? What are we forgetting? What needs to be remembered and cherished? What needs to be forgiven? What needs to be healed? What are the treasures hidden in our fields? What is waiting to be discovered?

There is an old story circling 'round that goes like this: Every time a child is born, an angel takes it under its wing and whispers divine secrets to it. The angel hints of its divine origin and fills its soul with mysteries from heaven. As the child grows, the angel's message remains buried in the depths of its being, evoking an infinite yearning in its soul. And so the child moves through life with a haunting memory of some hallowed truth once known but now forgotten.

The poet William Wordsworth speaks this same truth using different words:

> *Our birth is but a sleep and a forgetting:*
> *The Soul that rises with us, our life's Star,*
> *Hath had elsewhere its setting,*
> *And cometh from afar:*
> *Not in entire forgetfulness,*
> *And not in utter nakedness,*
> *But trailing clouds of glory do we come*

From God, who is our home:
Heaven lies about us in our infancy![1]

You are the child of this story and of this poem. A retreat is
a time to remember those sacred truths buried in your soul. Do
not try to force the remembering. Rather, quieten your soul that
God may teach you this ancient wisdom. There are some things
we can learn only in silence.

The human heart longs for the divine! Now is the time to recognize this longing for what it is—an invitation to spiritual growth.
More and more people are beginning to pay attention to this invitation and are searching out spiritual centers for retreats.

Frequently retreatants will say at the end of a retreat I'm leading, "Oh, this has been so nourishing—and now, back to *real
life!*" This is said in a tone that suggests real life isn't very nourishing. By real life, of course, they are talking about life with all
its daily struggles. Pondering this dreaded dailiness, I am reminded
of something a retreat guide once said to me, "What you do daily,
you do dully, *unless you do it deeply,* which you seldom do!"

This book will support your longing to do the daily things
deeply. It is a book for spiritual maintenance—to help you inte-
grate the fruits of your retreat into daily life.

To further illustrate the purpose of this book I want to share
with you a memory. Long ago when I was learning to type, I used
to delight in typing letters to my friends without pressing the space
bar. Now when you don't press the space bar, you've got a real
mess, and there is much decoding to be done. It is the *spaces in
between* that enable us to understand the message.

Life is very much the same. It is the spaces in between that
help us understand life. But, you see, some of us keep forgetting
to press the space bar. And why do we forget? Well, many of us
have the disease that some doctors are calling *hurry sickness.*[2]
I am offering you a way of recovering from your hurry sickness.
Here is a way to press the space bar. There may be times when
you will have the luxury of pressing the space bar for a whole

week, but many people are not able to make an extended retreat. That is the reason for this book: with it as a guide, you can make a retreat in your home.

The Song of the Seed is an at-home retreat. The seed is the Word of God, and the song is your daily life centered around this Word. The parable of the sower and the seed from Luke's Gospel is the text for your retreat. The Sower (God) believes in the land of your heart and wants to be intimately involved in the daily, dusty ordinariness of your life.

The Word who came bounding from that royal throne in the heavens wants to be immersed in your life (Wisdom 18:14).

The Word who became flesh wants to dwell within you and live all around you (John 1:14).

That Word of God who is alive and active, piercing and discerning, wants you to come out of hiding and bear the pain and joy of being known (Hebrews 4:12).

The Word of God by whom the heavens were made wants to continue the work of creation in you (Psalm 19:2).

The seed that is the Word of God wants to be sown in the land of your heart (Luke 8:11).

Because the Word of God is to be your guide during this retreat, you will be given a Scripture passage to pray with each day. I invite you to approach each text as a *songline* that has the power to lead you back to the original wisdom the angel whispered in your ear.

Songlines are part of the sacred belief of the Australian aborigines. These people believe that the wisdom and knowledge of their ancestors are like invisible footprints, sacred tracks through their land, which they call songlines. By finding the right songline, they can connect with their ancestors.

In the beginning, the Great Ancestors sang the world into existence. Thus, these people believe that part of their task in life is to help keep the world created. All of their songs, their works of art, their tending of creation is their way of making real what is already present. Their lifework is to continue *singing up the country.*[3]

During this retreat seeds will be sown in the land of your heart. These seeds, wisdom from the Scriptures, are like footprints linking you to the One who is continually singing you into new life. The Word of God bounding from the heavens to the earth leaves an invisible trail that is part of your salvation history. It is your personal songline—*your connection to the Divine Sower.*

Just as there are seeds in the soil, so too there are secrets in the soil. The right seed touching the right secret can produce an abundance of new life. Your task during this retreat, then, is to tend the soil of your soul that it may be a place where the seed can bear fruit.

To help you make a connection between the land of your heart and the land of the earth, I will use symbols of the earth for your daily prayer exercises: the sower and the seed, the sowing, the fallow season, reaping, and gleaning.

At times life can seem like a vast, barren wilderness with no order, nothing but land unexplored. Land uncultivated! No country at all! In Willa Cather's lovely pioneer novel, *My Antonia*, Jim, the narrator of the story, reminisces about the day he came to the barren land of Nebraska as a little boy.

> I slipped from under the buffalo hide, got up on my knees and peered over the side of the wagon. There seemed to be nothing to see; no fences, no creeks or trees, no hills or fields . . . there was nothing but land; not a country at all, but the material out of which countries are made.[4]

During this retreat, try to look at the barren spaces of your life as the original emptiness out of which creation takes place. Are you willing to give the Sower a chance to sing up the country of your heart? And after the songs have been sung in the land of your heart, will you continue the song and so continue to make real the creation of your life?

The first two chapters, "The Groundwork," will prepare you for your retreat. Chapter 1, "The Song of the Seed," is my personal reflection on Luke's Gospel of the sower and the seed. Chapter 2, "Romancing the Word," suggests a process for praying with the Word of God each day. I hope these chapters will motivate you, preparing your soil for the seed to be sown.

Your retreat is divided into three ten-day sessions entitled "Bending," "Mending," and "Tending." You may need longer than ten days, because this is an at-home retreat. Set your own pace.

Forming a Retreat Group

Although this retreat has been designed as an individual journey for you, a daily experience to pray through *alone,* you may find it helpful to include others. When you decide to use *The Song of the Seed* for your personal prayer, invite some friends or members of your church to discuss with you ways to use this book—alone and together.

My suggestion is that you form a retreat group of six to ten people. Each of you read through the introduction and the first two chapters alone. When you are ready to begin the retreat exercises, have an opening meeting to decide upon a block of time that will fit your respective schedules. For example, you may decide to use two or three weeks for your first ten-day session. Move through the retreat exercises at a comfortable pace, in your own home and *alone.* Some in the group may need two days for each exercise; others may prefer just one day. Your daily schedules will determine the pace.

I have prepared a group experience for you to use at the end of each ten-day session. When all members of your group have finished the first retreat, choose a day to come together for praying and sharing the fruits of your experience. You may want to choose an evening block of time in someone's home, or you may wish to meet at a church or a retreat center for a longer period.

These meetings can be times of prayerful bonding and group commitment as well as times for setting dates for future sessions.

If your group is meeting in the evening, you may want to use several evenings as opposed to just one, so as not to cut short or omit the faith sharing and contemplative sitting. Keep in mind that in planning the group session I considered the probability that some groups will want to use a whole day for their gathering. With spaces in between for silent reflection, this would be possible. Thus, I have provided a goodly amount of material.

Suggestions for Group Prayer and Sharing

The first thing you need is someone to take the lead in preparing for your group experience. The leader may be the one who initially took the responsibility to form the retreat group. Or, this person may wish to ask for a volunteer to lead or co-lead one of the three group sessions.

Each prayer session will require some researching and gathering of materials. There will be music to be purchased or borrowed. Some instructions may have to be given to the group ahead of time. All of this suggests that someone must plan and facilitate the group's time together. Choosing a leader is your first task. Or, perhaps volunteering to be the leader is your first task.

I encourage the leader to use his or her own options in planning this prayer. Always feel free to substitute music, songs, symbols, and rituals that you are familiar with if the ones I have suggested pose a problem for you. The prayer experience I have planned is yours to use in whatever way seems best for your group. You may wish to delete or revise some of my suggestions.

The leader should meet with one of the participants to review the prayer service before each group gathering. This is the time to consider any details that need your attention before your group meeting. Readers will need to be chosen. As the leader, you may wish to delegate someone to facilitate the faith sharing or the period of contemplative sitting. All decisions should be made before the group meeting so that your gathering can be a time of prayerful leisure.

Guidelines for Contemplative Sitting

During this ten-day retreat, you will be given some directives for individual periods of *contemplative sitting*. Thus, when you come to your group session the practice of communal contemplative sitting may be new to you. It is a healing way of emptying your mind and just *being in God* together.

An excellent way to ease the group into this contemplative way of being together is by means of meditative music. Begin with soft instrumental music. Gradually turn the volume down until it is no longer audible. When you wish to bring the group back to attention, slowly turn the volume up again.

Guidelines for Faith Sharing

For each session of group prayer, I suggest some space for *faith sharing*. In this simple way of telling one another how you are encountering God in the Scriptures and in your life, the ideal is to listen reverently without commenting on one another's sharing. This way of listening guards against the temptation of trying to "fix" one another or give advice. In other words, this is not so much a discussion as a prayerful way of being together. It is a breaking of your stories and insights, your sorrows and joys, with one another. A loving attentiveness is the finest gift you have to offer the one who is sharing. And the very best advice I have to give you is a Native American saying: *Listen, or your tongue will keep you deaf!*

I encourage you to be creative in your planning. Take risks. Listen to one another. Give the Divine Sower lots of freedom to sing up the country of your heart.

The
Groundwork

CHAPTER I

The Song of the Seed

The farmer waits
for the precious crop
from the earth,
being patient with it
until it receives
the early and the late rains.
You also must be patient.
Strengthen your hearts,
for the coming of the Lord is near.

James 5:7–8

The earth is a mother. Her soil has soul. She blesses each seed that is sown, and the seed becomes a song. From the altar of her womb we are fed.

The sower is the priest or priestess offering the seed to mother earth. The poet is the one who understands this best:

As I kneel to put the seeds in
careful as stitching, I am in love.
You are the bed we all sleep on.
You are food we eat, the food
we ate, the food we will become.
We are walking trees rooted in you . . .

I worship on my knees, laying
the seeds in you, that worship

> *rooted in need, in hunger, in kinship,*
> *flesh of the planet with my own flesh,*
> *a ritual of compost, a litany of manure. . . .*[1]

My ancestors were people of the soil. Memories of the way of the earth are etched in my soul. I have always felt a unique kinship with the land. Perhaps this is why the parable of the sower and the seed holds a special enchantment for me.

The artist Vincent van Gogh felt this enchantment also. He was charmed by the magic of memories of the past. For him, the sower was a symbol of longing for the infinite. The idea of a sower forever haunted him and gave birth to his many paintings of the Sower.

I am using the parable of the sower and the seed as the text for your retreat. A splendid parallel can be found in the seed falling into the soil and the seed of the Word of God falling into your soul.

The seed is the Word of God. Many seeds have already been sown in you. Many songs have been sung through you because of your faithfulness to the Word. The song of the seed is the continuous prayer of your daily life—your life in process.

The "longing for the infinite" that van Gogh spoke of resides in every human heart. At times you may wonder about the origin of this longing. Could it be part of the mystery whispered to you by the angel at your birth? Is it one of the seeds sown in you trying to sing its way through your soil?

It seems to be a mixture of joy and sadness, love and fear, loneliness and contentment; yet when you try to name it, all words limp. It has taken up residence in the depths of your being, and it refuses to be silent.

This infinite longing that stirs in the depths of your soul is a spark of the divine. It is one of the seeds that has fallen into your life. It may be a seed that was sown many years ago. You will be restless with longing until you listen to its song.

As you prepare for your retreat, reflect on this paraphrase of the parable of the sower and the seed. Variations of the text can be found in Luke 8:4–15, Matthew 13:1–23, and Mark 4:1–20.

A sower went out to sow some seed. As the seed was sown, some fell on *the edge of the path* and was trampled on; the birds of the air ate it up. Some seed fell on *rocky ground,* and when it came up it withered, having no moisture. Some seed fell *among thorns;* the thorns grew with it and choked it. And some seed fell into *good soil;* it grew and produced a hundredfold (NRSV, paraphrased).

This is a story about the passion of an extravagantly lavish sower. Having grown up on a farm, I remember enough about sowing seed to know that one doesn't cast out seeds willy-nilly as this sower did. It is true there is a method of scattering seeds called broadcasting, but even when you are broadcasting you stay out of the briars, rocks, and pathways.

We know, of course, that the sower Jesus speaks of in this parable is a loving Father, a nurturing Mother. This is our God, the Divine Sower, who is so intent on getting the Word out that the possibility of losing a few seeds among the thorns and rocks is a small matter. Hope is the force behind this sowing. This is a sower who trusts the soil—who believes that the soil has soul. Thus the seed is cast out with wild abandon.

So what happens to all the seeds that this trusting Sower keeps broadcasting in our lives? Why do they not all take root? Why does each seed not become a song? The poet Tagore wondered about a similar problem many years ago. Let's take a look at his musings to see if they might correspond to the questions of our hearts.

> *I know not how thou singest, my master!*
> *I ever listen in silent amazement.*
>
> *The light of thy music illumines the*
> *world. The life breath of thy music runs*
> *from sky to sky. The holy stream of thy*
> *music breaks through all stony obstacles*
> *and rushes on.*
>
> *My heart longs to join in thy song, but*
> *vainly struggles for a voice. I would speak*

> *but speech breaks not into song, and I cry out*
> *baffled. Ah, thou has made my heart captive*
> *in the endless meshes of my music, my master![2]*

I, too, have felt captive in the middle of my song. I have felt the sadness of something holy trapped in my reluctant soil. The seed full of promise falls into my life, yet something prevents the seed from becoming a song.

Returning to the parable of the Sower, let us consider the journey of the seed. There was nothing wrong with the seed or the soil. The problem was an adversary in the soil.

As you begin your retreat, reflect on obstacles to the seed's growth in your life. Look at your soil. Some of the seed fell on the pathways, some on rocky ground or in briars. Some seed fell on good soil. Taking each of these in turn, I will share with you my observations about the obstacles in my own life. You may wish to do the same in your retreat group.

The Edge of the Path

On a pathway one can expect traffic. It is a place that is trodden upon. The feet of joggers, runners, walkers wear the path down. Bikes and other vehicles continue to stir up the dust. If the seed is sown here, it is likely to be lost in a whirl of activity or trodden underfoot. It cannot take root, break open, and stretch toward the sun, for it is always beaten down again. The traffic prevents its growth.

Sometimes this happens to the Word of God in my life. I hang around the edge of the path too much. The traffic, which I both detest and love, prevents the seed from taking root in me. It is not the birds of the air that steal away God's Word; it is all the activity on the pathway. I linger near the road's edge because I don't want to miss anything. As a result, I miss the Word of God trying to penetrate the ground of my being.

On the edge of the path I am torn by distractions.

The Rocky Ground

It always amazes me when I see a plant or flower, or sometimes even a little tree, growing out of rock. It seems like a miracle. Even in rock the seed can sometimes find moisture and space to grow. The problem with growing in the rocks, however, is that the root system is not deep. Thus the little plant is at the mercy of the elements. Winds, rains, and ice tend to force it out of its shallow home. It can easily be uprooted.

There is a lesson for me here in this rocky ground. If the Word of God is to find a home in me, it must put down its roots deep into my being. And so I must guard myself from being a shallow person. There are rocks in my life that make it difficult for the Word to become rooted in me. Sometimes they seem more like boulders. They range anywhere from bitterness, selfishness, and jealousy to a casual, passionless attitude about growth. They are dangerous barriers to the root system that the Word of God needs for mature growth. As I pray with my rocky soil, I see the need to clear away the obstacles that harden my heart and keep me shallow. I pray for a deep root system so that every little wind won't topple me over.

On the rocky ground I wither for lack of depth.

Among the Thorns

The greatest thieves in my life are found among the thorns. The seed falls into the soil of my soul, yet the Word of God does not grow up in me. It does not reach maturity. The Word does not become flesh. The Seed does not become a song. This Word of God, this powerful seed of potential, is smothered by the countless worries and concerns of my life.

To speak in painfully plain language, I do not make the Word of God a high priority. Disappointing as it is to hear myself admit this out loud, it is a wound in me that I need to understand.

Day by day I give the thorns a place of preeminence in my life. Of course it is foolish, yet I seem to be content with this foolishness. I allow the anxieties and worries of each day to crowd out my presence to the Word of God. Unhealthy attachments to my own will, a clinging to possessions, devotion to my own agenda, too much dependence on friends, the careful guarding of my time—all these are among the thorns that smother the life of the seed that has fallen into my soil. The roots of my own will become a large entanglement of briars. On some days they even choke out my deep longing to be rooted in Christ—a yearning that I thought would never leave me.

I do want the Word of God to find a home in me, but when I refuse to surrender my idols the seed cannot become a song. Among the thorns I am smothered by unhealthy attachments.

These, then, are the obstacles to the seed's growth in my life: my attraction to distractions, my lack of depth, and my unhealthy attachments.

The Good Soil

But wait! There is something in me that is not content to hang about directionless along the edge of the path. There is a thirst in me so deep it will move aside the rocks, seeking moisture. There is a yearning that is intense in its desire to put God first. It may take a lifetime, but I have no doubt this unnameable mystery within, the seed that fell at the beginning of creation, will finally crowd out the thorns. Yes, there is One who believes in me enough to continue singing up the country of my heart.

The seeds sown in our lives are, in reality, seeds of our potential. They are sparks of the divine. They must take root in the earthiness of our lives and grow. It is essential for us to remember that the sower in our parable did not experience only obstacles. Some of the seed fell into good soil and yielded fruit a hundredfold.

In this retreat I want you to focus on your good soil. Your soil may be very unwilling to receive the seed at certain times. The deeper truth, however, is your readiness to be nurtured by the Word of God. Perhaps you have never affirmed your openness to spiritual growth. God can do wonders in a heart that is open. You already possess this openness or you wouldn't be reading this book.

Pause for a moment and be grateful for your open heart.

As you begin this journey, then, believe that you have within you all that is needed to nurture the seeds that fall into your life. During this retreat, a special seed will be sown in your life each day. The Sower and I will work together searching for the right seed. I ask only that, in spite of the barriers, you keep remembering your good soil and your open heart. If you hold these truths in your memory, the obstacles will not be able to crowd out the Word of God.

In the next chapter you will be given a process for praying with the seed—the Word of God (lectio divina).

CHAPTER 2

Romancing the Word

Humbly
welcome the Word
which has been planted
in you
and can save
your souls.

James 1:21, NJB

We are surrounded by the Word of God. It permeates us like the air we breathe. It challenges us to walk with discerning hearts in the company of God.

How can we grow in wisdom so as to live attentive to this creative Word of God? The psalmist cries out, "In the secret of my heart teach me wisdom" (Psalm 51, Grail). Down through the years we echo that cry—a songline from the hearts of our ancestors to our own hearts, a songline from their notebooks to ours.

We are taught this wisdom through sustained periods of deep reflection and loving attention to the Word. A much-loved monastic way of attending the Word of God is *lectio divina* (LEX-see-o dee-VEE-nah). During this retreat you will be using the discipline of lectio divina; literally, "divine reading." Lectio is a way of reading with the heart. It is a contemplative way of reflecting on the Scriptures or other spiritual classics.

Haste is the enemy of reflection. Lectio does not allow us to hurry. It is impossible to hurry through a text if you are reading with the heart. In this age of speed, how tempting it is to read in a driven manner. All too often getting finished with the reading, rather than being transformed by the Word, becomes the goal.

The practice of lectio divina guides us to the inner work that brings about transformation. It requires a deep listening to the Word planted in our souls. It summons us to a tender abiding in the hidden mystery of God. It asks of us a patient waiting for God's personal revelation of truth to us. It draws us into a loving romance with the One who rules the world from the throne of our hearts.[3] It encourages in us a joyful expectation of the healing touch of the Beloved. A deep listening! A tender abiding! A patient waiting! A loving romance! A joyful expectation! These are the warm invitations of this gentle way of being with the Word of God. The gift of this intimate way of praying does not come in one sitting. It is a daily discipline requiring faithful practice.

Long ago when I was a novice in monastic life, I would get up before the crack of dawn and trudge sleepily to our monastery chapel to pray the Divine Office with my sisters. Together we would climb through the psalms: praising God, rejoicing, pleading, complaining, yearning, crying out, thanking.

In our daily classes we were assured that if we were faithful to the Word we would be drawn more deeply into relationship with God, making our morning treks to the chapel a delight. In our daily pondering of the Scriptures, we were asked to listen with the *ear of the heart*. It was all very romantic at first, but the crack of dawn began coming too soon. The romance wore off. I am happy to say that now, in my middle years, the romance is returning. I am beginning to see lectio divina as a way to *romance the Word*.

Romancing the Word

When you romance the Word, you pursue the Word as it pursues you. You ponder it, pray it, sing it, study it, love it. You treasure it as Mary treasured the mysteries unfolding in her life (Luke

2:19–20). Listen to it with the ear of your heart. Cling to it as to a beloved. Cherish it. Become a home for it.

Follow it as you would follow a sacred pathway. Let it be a *songline* leading you to the hidden riches of your soul's original wisdom—that mysterious wisdom that the angel whispered to you at birth.

In the Gospel of Luke we find the disciples of Jesus romancing the Word. We are told that when Jesus taught in the Temple, the religious leaders wanted to put him to death. They could find no way to accomplish this, though, because the people were *hanging on his words* (Luke 19:47–48, NAB). How different our lives might be if it could be said of us that we were hanging on the Word of God.

As the Sower begins to sow the seeds of God's Word in your heart during this retreat, I offer you a way of being present to these seeds. The way is lectio divina—romancing the Word.

A Guide for Your Romance

In this guide for romancing the Word, I will lead you in a way of praying the Scriptures that has become a creative pattern for my life.

Lectio divina is a way of plowing up the field of your soul. In the guide below, I have compared movements of life in the soil with movements of grace in the soul.

The six elements listed below have come out of my many years of faithfulness to lectio divina. Please observe that the descriptive phrase on the left pertains to tending the soil, while the corresponding phrase on the right applies to tending the soul.

The Fallow Season	Quieting the Soul
The Sowing of the Seed	Reflective Reading
Resting in the Soil	Contemplative Sitting
The Reaping	Meditation
The Song of the Seed	Prayer
Gleanings	Journaling

These are the six elements you will use throughout your retreat. On each new day I will give you the theme for the day in a few sentences under the heading Focus for the Day. After glancing at the focus you will be ready to move into this pattern for your prayer, lectio divina.

I now offer you a more detailed explanation of each of the above elements. Return to this Guide for Your Romance until you are familiar with this pattern for your prayer.

The Fallow Season: Quieting the Soul

> Be still, and know
> that I am God!
>
> Psalm 46:10

Just as the soil must, at times, lay fallow, so too, the soul must rest. You may have been told that idleness is the work of the devil. Wrong! Give yourself the gift of some idle moments. It is time to prepare your soil by doing nothing. Sit with the hallowed ground of your being. Allow the natural flow of your breath to rise and fall as you await the sowing of the seed. Relax. Quiet your soil. Quiet your soul.

This stance of tranquil receptivity is a very important first step for your journey with the Word each day. One of the obstacles to communion with God is a cluttered mind. A cluttered mind suggests a divided heart—a fragmentation. Communion with God suggests an undivided heart—two loves uniting. So, yearn for the kind of emptiness that has no room for clutter. Room for nothing save the Beloved! Pray silently, ". . . it is no longer I who live, but it is Christ who lives in me" (Gal. 2:20). Rest in this truth.

I suggest at least five minutes for this time of silent preparation. Eventually experience will teach you the time frame that works best for you. This is your fallow season as you wait for the sowing of the seed. Put aside your book now, and silence the land of your heart.

The Sowing of the Seed: Reflective Reading

It is seed-sowing time. Just as the sower's seed falls into the soil, the seed of the Word of God falls into your soul. Each day you will be given a Scripture text to romance. This will be your first reading of the Word. Read contemplatively, slowly, and when possible, aloud. This is not a time for discursive meditation or active pondering of the text. This is your *deep listening* time. It is a time for lingering. Stroll through the words as if you were meandering through a garden. Focus on the good soil of your life and its potential to nourish the seed that has been sown. Perhaps some little plants are already pushing through your soil. Perhaps some buds are beginning to open into flowers. Gaze gratefully at the flowers as you stroll, remembering, though, that it is not time to pick the flowers. This first reading is more like a walk through a botanical garden.

Reading slowly and lingering is often difficult for us fast movers. Try to remember that your goal is not to get finished with the reading but to be transformed by the Word. Read with a listening heart. Read with the ear of your heart. "Humbly welcome the Word which has been planted in you and can save your souls" (James 1:21, NJB).

Resting in the Soil: Contemplative Sitting

If you are acquainted with the lectio process, you will notice that I have rearranged the order of this classic model for praying with the Word of God. I am placing your period of contemplation immediately after your first reading and before your meditation. It seems to follow naturally that after the seed is planted in the soil there be a gestation phase—a time of waiting for growth, for birth, for the harvest. During this phase, we try to surrender control by means of contemplative sitting. You have done what you can to wake up your soil. Now you need to let God have you. It is time for a patient waiting and a tender abiding. You are entering into the wordless prayer of being held by God. In this prayer of total surrender, try to let go of all words except the one great Word. Remember, it is no longer you who live; it is Christ who lives in you. Christ will do just fine living in you. Your task is just to *be there*. You are a vessel of emptiness for Christ to abide in.

Contemplative sitting is a time for the Word to become flesh in you. Let your images of God go. Let your thoughts about God go. You are simply resting in God and God is resting in you. "Abide in me as I abide in you" (John 15:4). Abide! Dwell! Rest! This holy rest of contemplative union with God will be the great prize of your life. Out of this union, you will be led back into the marketplace to give your life away again.

In her novel *O Pioneers!,* Willa Cather reminds us of our need to believe in the good soil of our lives, to do what we can to wake it up and then to wait. Alexandria has taken charge of the farm after her father's death. Her brothers are not very enthusiastic about the wild land that they must tame, and, Carl, a neighbor and friend, gives up completely and moves to the city. Many years later he returns for a visit and is amazed at what Alexandria has done to the land. At one point in the story she says to him,

> We hadn't any of us much to do with it. The land did it. It had its little joke. It pretended to be poor because nobody knew how to work it right; and then all at once it worked itself. It woke up out of its sleep and stretched itself and it was so big, so rich, that we suddenly found we were rich, just from sitting still.[4]

You and I can learn the same lesson from sitting still with the land of the heart. It, too, has its little jokes. We think it is poor soil because we don't know how to work it. When we learn to do our inner work, it will wake up and work itself. So you see, truly, all we need is *a patient waiting* and *a tender abiding.*

I will not give you a lot of directions for this time of contemplation. The only way to learn is by sitting still. Only practice perfects the art of contemplation. I will offer you a tiny poem as a guide to begin this quiet time, to center you in Christ each day. I suggest about twenty minutes for this period of contemplative sitting. If at first this seems too long, you can begin with a shorter time and gradually add to it. It may be helpful to set a small, gentle alarm so you will not have to worry about watching the clock and thus will be free to rest in God without anxiety.

The Reaping: Meditation

Sow saving justice for yourselves,
reap a harvest of faithful love;
break up your fallow ground:
it is time to seek out Yahweh . . .

Hosea 10:12, NJB

Having rested with the Word, you are now ready to interact with it. Return to the beginning of the text and read through it again. This is your second reading of the Word. During this process of meditation, you become a reaper. You harvest the fruit of the seed that has been sown in your life. Each seed holds a gift. The gift is revealed to you in the form of new insights and challenges. Often new questions emerge. This meditation becomes a time for praying those questions and reflecting on the message the text offers for your personal growth.

During your meditation continue listening to the Word. This time, however, become actively involved with the Word. Remember the flower that you gazed upon in your first reading? You may now pick that flower. Hold it. Study it. Listen to it. The plants that were only peeping out of the soil during your stroll through the garden are now ready to be gathered. This is a time of integration.

You are involved in *a loving romance* with the Word of God. This romance will, at times, involve a bittersweet struggle, for you may see things about yourself that you would rather not see. You are being called to conversion and so to pain and love. You will often feel both vulnerable and grateful.

In my own life I often find myself running from my insights. Though there is a part of me that truly wants to see, another part would just as soon remain blind. Seeing with new eyes calls for transformation. I wrestle with the Word and its meaning for my life as Jacob wrestled with the angel. If, like Jacob, I come out of this struggle with the wound of healthy pain and a new name, there is reason to hope. The wound implies that something in me has been pierced and I will never be the same again. The piercing may come in the form of a new insight—an insight that leaves me vulnerable and grateful.

In this stage of your romance with the Word, then, you are called to reap the harvest of the seed's growth in your soil.

In your daily guide for each ten-day retreat I will ask you to consider some meditation points. At the end of your meditation, choose a *songline* to lead you through the day. Your songline can be a word or phrase gleaned from your reflection—a little prayer enabling the Word to continue singing up the country of your heart throughout the day. I will be sharing with you the songline that has risen out of my own prayer. On some days the one I choose may seem right for you also. On others, you may wish to choose your own.

The Song of the Seed: Prayer

The "Song of the Seed" is your personal response to the Word of God. It is the continuation of your loving romance with the Word. In reading and meditation you listened attentively to God speaking to you. In contemplation you put away your thoughts and concerns and simply rested in God. Now it is time for God to listen to you. Use this time as a short period of prayer to speak your heart to God in any way you wish. Your prayer may take the form of praise, thanksgiving, petition, repentance. Or, you may speak to God without words—in sacred gestures, acts of love, tears, or ardent yearning. You may write your prayer, dance your prayer, sing your prayer. Or, your prayer may take the form of a slow, meditative walk.

Then, let your prayer lead you through the day. Use your songline to assist you. Carry with you *a joyful expectation* of the continued healing touch of the Beloved. Take the Word with you to the office, to the factory, to the classroom, to the kitchen, to the streets and fields. Stop occasionally and hold dear the memory of the seed that was sown. When you see a flower bending in the breeze, remember, what you see is the fruit of a seed. The seed that falls into the depths of the soil eventually grows into a plant that is visible to you. It is the song of the seed—earth's prayer in living color.

So too, the seed that falls into your soul slowly becomes a song. It is the song of God's life in you, the Word becoming visible in you. It is the song of the seed—the prayer of your life in living color. It will continue to sing up the country of your soul.

Although I share my personal prayer with you in your retreat exercises, I trust you will allow your own prayer to arise.

Gleanings: Journaling

A gleaner is one who walks through the fields and gardens gathering what has been left by the reapers. At the end of your day, spend a few moments being a gleaner. Walk back through your day of harvesting the Word of God. Let this be a kind of review of life. Now that the sun is setting, ask yourself, Does anything come together in a clearer picture? Is there anything I missed? Did I remember my songline during the day? How does this day of creation feel in my heart? Has this day been, for me, a deep listening, a patient waiting, a tender abiding, a loving romance, and a joyful expectation?

Use whatever you need to help you in your gleanings: insights and memories, poems, prayers, songs, ideas, quotes from other sowers and gleaners. Record some of your gleanings in your journal. After you have spent time with your own journaling, read my journal entry.

The path of lectio divina I have just walked through with you will help water the seed planted in your soil. However, the real goal of lectio is learning to live your life quietly and naturally around the Word of God at every moment. In this way all your works throughout the day are enhanced. You are living as one absorbed in God yet very much in touch with the world about you.

In her book of life, Saint Teresa of Avila lists four ways of watering the garden, signifying ways that God visits the soul in prayer. The first way is simply to draw water from the well. This is rather laborious and could perhaps represent our wordiness in prayer. The second way is to use a water wheel and buckets when the water is drawn by a windlass. In this way you get more water with less labor. Her third way is to plant the garden by a stream. The ground is naturally saturated with water, and one does not need to water it so often. The fourth way she describes is God's sending of a good rain.[5]

Of Teresa's four ways of watering the garden, the third way best describes the prayer of lectio. The psalmist echoes the same cry: "You are blessed if you are like a tree planted near streams of water" (Psalm 1). This is the way of lectio: to teach you to live by the water streams. As you carry the Word with you throughout the day, your life becomes permeated with God's presence. You become the Word, the song of the seed.

After sharing this guide for romancing the Word with you, I feel drawn to offer a caution. In no way am I trying to chain you to a formula for prayer. Use what is helpful. You will eventually find your own rhythm and style. I am simply offering you a way to live your life around the Word of God. I am asking you to sit beside the water streams.

The most important points to remember are these:

1. The ground of your being is holy; relax in it! Breathe deeply. Quieten your soul. Wait patiently.

2. Read the Word slowly. This requires a deep listening.

3. Put all words and thoughts aside as you rest in the Beloved: a patient waiting, a tender abiding. You are absorbed in God.

4. Continue your deep listening in a loving romance with the Word. This romance may include a bittersweet encounter, a lover's struggle, as you are slowly taught by God.

5. Move through the day in joyful expectation of becoming the song of the seed. You live by the water streams of the Word of God. Your songline is your companion. Ever so slowly, your daily life becomes a blessing.

6. At the end of your day, take a loving glance at the fruits of your prayer, and spend a little time journaling. Bless your day and sleep in peace.

You are now ready to begin your first ten days of romancing the Word. Have you invited other seekers to join you on this journey?

PART I

Bending: The Dance

When true simplicity
is gained
to bow and to bend
we will not be ashamed
To turn, to turn will be our delight
Till by turning, turning
we come 'round right.

As you begin your first ten days of romancing the Word, clothe yourself with the natural reverence that comes from an awareness of the sacred within and around you. The gesture of *bending* suggests an attitude of radical surrender. Look at these days as an invitation to bend to the God of your life. I envision the act of bending as a kind of dance—a dance of obedience to the breath of life in you. Each day will be like learning a new step to the dance.

Bowing will be part of your daily ritual. The gesture of bowing is an exterior sign of an awesome presence you are encountering. Begin your day by bowing to the dawn. A deep bow gives witness to the truth that you are awake and ready to receive the new day. All too often we *take* the day rather than receive it.

To help you see the beauty of these movements as part of your daily prayer, I share with you a story from a Japanese Zen master:

> People often ask me how Buddhists answer the question, "Does God exist?"
>
> The other day I was walking along the river. The wind was blowing. Suddenly I thought, oh! the air really exists. We know that the air is there, but unless the wind blows against our face, we are not aware of it. Here in the wind I was suddenly aware, yes it's really there.
>
> And the sun too. I was suddenly aware of the sun, shining through the bare trees. Its warmth, its brightness, all this completely free, completely gratuitous. Simply there for us to enjoy.
>
> And without my knowing it, completely spontaneous, my two hands came together, and I realized that I was making gassho. And it occurred to me that this is all that matters: that we can bow, take a deep bow. Just that. Just that.[1]

A deep bow! A prayer of adoration! A loving awareness of the sacred! This is the spirit I want to instill in you throughout this retreat. The beautiful words of the well-known Shaker folk song "Simple Gifts" captures this spirit. You are probably familiar with this song; you may find yourself humming or singing the words rather than just reading them.

'Tis a gift to be simple,
'tis a gift to be free,
'tis a gift to come down
where we ought to be.
And when we find ourselves
in the place just right,
'Twill be in the valley of
love and delight.
When true simplicity is gain'd
To bow and to bend we shan't
be asham'd.
To turn, turn will be our delight
Till by turning, turning, we
come 'round right.

These musical words call forth the image of a graceful dance, a prayerful movement of bowing and bending to the sacred life around you and within you. Begin your prayer each morning by playing the song "Simple Gifts." Purchase a recording in a music store or borrow a copy from a friend. (See the list of resources at the end of the book.)

May these ten days be, for you, days of obedience and openness, days of welcoming the seed and romancing the Word. May each day teach you a new step to the dance of life.

It may be helpful during these next days to return periodically to "The Groundwork" and review the section "Romancing the Word."

CHAPTER I

Day 1—
The Dance of Trust

Focus for the Day

Bending to a childlike trust in God. Stop worrying; you are in God's hands. Dance, "Simple Gifts."

The Fallow Season

Silent preparation for the Word. This is the fallow season for your hallowed ground. Breathe deeply. Wait patiently.

The Sowing of the Seed

Read Matthew 6:25–34. Read carefully and slowly with the ear of your heart.

Resting in the Soil

Let this tiny poem guide you into the heart of God.

> *Like a wild flower*
> *in God's care*
> *I put my worries away*
> *trusting the One who holds me.*

The Reaping

Meditate on Matthew 6:25–34.

1. This text does not suggest that material possessions are evil. Rather, it is addressing priorities. How do your priorities need to be "turned 'round right"?
2. Spend some time reflecting on both trust and worry. Whom do you trust? What do you worry about?
3. Think of some way to celebrate your trust in God.

Songline

> Trust, rather than worry!

The Song of the Seed

Jesus, press deeply into my soil a seed of trust that, like the birds of the air, I may fly unfettered, a free child in love with life. Write on my heart the truth of your care for me, and let me discover that truth written there. Today let there be more trust and less worry in my life. Be my partner in the dance of trust so that all my priorities may turn 'round right. Astonish me with your loving presence. Guide me and guard me under the shadow of your wings. And should some dark shadow cross my life, even then teach me to trust.

> *May it come to pass!*

Gleanings

> *When I see a father or mother carrying a child, I am reminded of the dance of trust. In many ways I have been carried from birth. This evening I recall the many ways God has carried me. As I grow older, I am more aware of being carried.*

I am also aware of the need to trust when I feel no loving arms around me. At this stage in my life, I seem to be more faithful about "going off to the hills" to pray. My time alone creates in me a kind of reservoir—a storehouse of divine presence that is helpful when the dark times come. With fingers of faith, I hold on to God's hand in the darkness. It is risky to trust. I may give someone my heart, and they may leave town with it. Still, it is a risk I must take. I have noticed that, as I am able to trust other people, my trust in God increases. These thoughts go wandering 'round my mind as I glean through the pages of this day.

CHAPTER 2

Day 2— The Dance of the Good Shepherd

Focus for the Day

Bending to a shepherd's care. Surrender to the loving guidance of the One who walks through the dark valley with you.

The Fallow Season

Dwell in the Presence. No words please! Abide in love.

The Sowing of the Seed

Read Psalm 23.

Resting in the Soil

Let these words enfold you in the Shepherd's embrace.

> *Through the dark valley*
> *Beside restful waters*
> *Sustained by your love*
> *I abide.*

The Reaping

Meditate on Psalm 23.

1. For your journey today I am leading you to a very familiar psalm. Prayerfully move through it with a new heart. The twenty-third psalm is a prayer of trust in divine protection. Celebrate the gift of the Good Shepherd in your life. Let God be a shepherd leading you through the green meadows, sitting beside the stream with you. Come to life's banquet table, and honor the One who walks beside you and anoints you with healing oils.

2. Clear your mind and your heart with these questions. Has this psalm come true in my life? Have I experienced the intimacy of God's loving presence? Have these words remained just words for me, or have they become the Word? Have I spent enough time in the shepherd's green pasture to become a green pasture for someone else? How often do I sit beside the restful waters? Do I surrender to the One who leads me through the dark valleys, or do I try to lead myself? Have I remembered the goodness and kindness that follow me?

Songline

You guide me on the right paths.

The Song of the Seed

O shepherd God—hear my prayer. Your forgetful child is praying. Lead me into the meadows of remembering. For even when I am in deep trouble I still try to lead. I have a tendency to forget your nearness. I forget the green meadows and the restful waters. I forget the banquet table. I forget the many times you have anointed me with the oil of your devoted guidance. I ignore the gift of your presence and try to do things on my own. Come again into the places of my heart where I most need you. Let me hear anew the song of the seed of your protecting presence. O Shepherd God, companion me on all the journeys of my life. Dance through the darkness with me.

May it come to pass!

Gleanings

It has been good to drink at the streams of the shepherd psalm again. It is such a lovely affirmation of presence. Once again I am reminded of the seeds that have been sown in my life. I can become green pastures and restful waters for others only if I am faithful in attending the green pastures and restful waters of my own life.

At times I feel I've lost the combination to my heart. I wander around in neglected meadows trying to find my way back home. At times like these, praying the Good Shepherd psalm is like finding the right combination again. I am touched by the incredible images of tender mercy and presence. I feel called to be more attentive to God's mercy and presence leading me on the good path. I long to let go of the reins and allow God to shepherd me. The best way back into my heart is to be led by One who knows the way.

CHAPTER 3

Day 3—
The Dance of the Spirit

Focus for the Day

Bending and bowing to the One who guides you and leads you to truth, the Spirit of Jesus.

The Fallow Season

Honor the good soil of your soul so that the seed will have a fertile place to be sown. It is time for soul-resting.

The Sowing of the Seed

Read Mark 1:1–11. Read contemplatively.

Resting in the Soil

Use this little poem to help you become centered.

> *I breathe in God*
> *I breathe out God*
> *and in again,*
> *I rest in the Beloved!*

The Reaping

Meditate on Mark 1:1–11.

1. Recall your water baptism. Let the image of the church of your baptism come to your mind. Listen to the flowing water calling you into the family of God. Listen to the voice of the One who calls to Jesus (and to you), "You are my beloved; my favor rests on you." Because you have put on Christ, you can claim these words as also addressed to you. The word *beloved* is one of great intimacy. Deep within, allow yourself to hear the voice of God calling you by this name: *"Beloved."* How have you experienced God's favor?

2. Your water baptism only prepares a path for your baptism of fire, which completes your first baptism. In your text for today, John reminds you that you will meet Jesus on the path and he will baptize you with the Holy Spirit. How do you need to be more open to the Spirit? As Jesus continues to call you "Beloved," ask him to show you the areas of your life that are crying out to be renewed.

Songline

Beloved!

The Song of the Seed

Beloved One, once upon a time your saving waters rushed over me, claiming me as a part of the family of God. It has been a bittersweet struggle in this holy, human family. Now it is time for my baptism of fire. I have hidden in the darkness of my soil too long. Send your spirit into my heart today that I may be drawn into the fire of your love. Penetrate the weary ground of my being with your saving presence. Give me your heart of fire, and I will never again live halfheartedly in the family of God.

May it come to pass!

Gleanings

Truly, I felt like God's beloved today. I was envisioning the little town of Altus, Arkansas, and my childhood church, St. Mary's, where I was baptized. My songline, Beloved, had become a part of my breath. Suddenly I heard the Beloved say to me, "Go to your childhood baptismal font." Because I was spending some time at a hermitage less than an hour from that church, it was easy enough to obey my inner voice. I drove slowly to the church using my songline, Beloved, along the way.

Finally I stood before the baptismal font. I didn't use a lot of words. I just touched the font and called out names of people whom I knew had been baptized at that font: my family, relatives, classmates, old friends in the parish. The names came tumbling out like prayers from the heart of the Beloved. I knew that God was remembering this particular cell of the family of God in a special way.

I listened to Jesus saying my own name . . . singing up the country of my heart . . . a songline from God's heart to my own: "You are my beloved; on you my favor rests!" I left that holy place with a few tears and a heart renewed.

CHAPTER 4

Day 4—
The Dance of the Child

Focus for the Day

Bending to the child within. Have reverence for that which is youngest in you today and, perhaps, wisest. Sit at the feet of your child.

The Fallow Season

Practice deep breathing. As you prepare to receive your Word, go back in memory to those tender young roots of childhood.

The Sowing of the Seed

Read Mark 10:13–16 and Matthew 11:25.

Resting in the Soil

Let these consoling words lead you into loving union with God.

> *Like a weaned child*
> *on its mother's breast*
> *Tenderly*
> *On You I rest.*

The Reaping

Meditate on Mark 10:13–16 and Matthew 11:25.

1. Unfortunately childhood innocence does not last long these days. What is there about the innocence of your childhood that you would like restored? What qualities do you suppose Jesus was thinking of when he said that we must become like children to enter the kingdom?

2. When Jesus asks us to become like children, perhaps he is suggesting that we learn to take time for beauty, that we live with the taste of life in our mouths, that we approach life as gift rather than duty, mystery rather than dilemma, adventure rather than danger. Meditate on these things.

3. Touch the child within today. No matter how deep you may have buried the child, that child waits for you. She wants to be set free. He wants to be set free. Bend and bow to your inner child. Hear again the words of Jesus: "Let the children come to me."

Songline

Give me the heart of a child.

The Song of the Seed

Jesus, do you remember the questions I used to ask as a child—and how I never thought they were dumb, and how *after asking the questions* I would be satisfied again for a while and could easily go back to trusting? Do you remember how I trusted right in the middle of all the questions?

I like that memory, Jesus. Surely that childhood gift isn't lost forever! I would like, once again, to go on trusting in the midst of my questions. I want to sit at someone's feet again, believing all my questions are beneficial to the household.

Lord Jesus, restore that spirit in me!
May it come to pass!

Gleanings

When I was a child there were many things that didn't faze
me, things that bother me dreadfully now as an adult. Some of
these things were hot weather, cold weather, getting caught in
the rain, getting places on time, getting all my chores done. I
seldom worried about catching a cold or getting dirty. I didn't
worry about saying something that would sound silly—or crying if I was hurt. I always gave myself permission to daydream,
to do useless things and to talk to things that wouldn't talk
back. I always had time to play, and I never got bored.

I was more spontaneous—less inhibited—than I am now.
I was so delightfully involved in life that I didn't notice many
of the inconveniences that trouble me today. One last and very
important memory is that I spent a lot of time with creation.
I was aware of beauty without analyzing it. Although many of
these gifts are still alive in me today, the radiance that once was
mine has dimmed. I must make plans to allow the child to ani-
mate me again.

CHAPTER 5

Day 5—
The Dance of
the Dry Bones

Focus for the Day

Bending to your hidden life.

The Fallow Season

Listen to your breath. It is the sound of the Spirit of God breathing life into you. When the breath stops, you die.

The Sowing of the Seed

Read Ezekiel 37:1–14.

Resting in the Soil

May these few words create in you a sacred space for God.

> *In the valley of dry bones*
> *I await you, smiling*
> *trusting your breath*
> *to come seeking my hidden life.*

The Reaping

Meditate on Ezekiel 37:1–14.

1. At some point on your spiritual journey you will inevitably find yourself in the valley of dry bones. This can be a very lonely place. It may seem that all spiritual consolation has been drained from you. Keep company with one of your desolate experiences today. Believe in the life hidden in these dry bones. Practice a prayerful deep breathing, remembering the One whose breath you are borrowing.

2. In regard to this hidden life, I have stumbled upon a very helpful exercise. When my life drains away and I find myself despondent and fearful, I practice the Prayer of Quiet. I sit down and smile over my dry bones. It is a kind of wordless prophesy. In the sign language of a smile it says, "Dry bones, hear the Word of God." Try smiling over your dry bones today.

Songline

> *Breathe life into these dry bones.*

The Song of the Seed

Pray for a renewal of your spirit using the prayer of the four winds. Beginning with the north, turn to each direction and make your appeal to the Holy One. "The Lord Yahweh says this: Come from the four winds, breath; breathe on these dead, so that they come to life" (Ezekiel 37:9, NJB).

O Wind of the North, come bringing courage. Come with your power and give me the strength to endure. May I grow to appreciate your forceful breath. Take me down to the truth. Down! Down! Way down underneath my words, down there where the secrets are. Teach me to wait in the darkness without fear. If I wait long enough, some day you will breathe me up again, bringing the secrets with me. O Wind of the North, come with your courage.

O Wind of the East, come bringing a rebirth of hope. Come with your morning sunlight. Immerse me in the ritual of rising. Come dancing into my dry bones. Come singing songs of resurrection. O Wind of the East, come with your rebirth of hope.

O Wind of the South, come bringing the energy of your love. Come singing up the country of my heart. Draw me into new possibilities for growth. Absorb me in the green journey of abundant life. Surprise me with your glory. O Wind of the South, come with the energy of your love.

O Wind of the West, come bringing transformation. Wrap me in mystery, and instill in me a yearning for the unknown. Caress me with your sweet breezes, and teach me to surrender. Startle me with the beauty of glorious sunsets, and give me a poet's heart. Comfort me with a death that calls me home. O Wind of the West, come with your transformation.

May it come to pass!

Gleanings

How important it is to listen to the life that hides in the cracks! How vital to that life, to believe in the dance hidden in the dry bones! A poet says it like this:

> *. . . but just when*
> *the old heap of bones*
> *seems most dry*
> *and deserted,*
> *a strong Breath of Life*
> *stirs among my dead.*
>
> *Someone named God*
> *comes to my fragments*

and asks, with twinkling eye:
"May I have this dance?"

the Voice stretches into me,
a stirring leaps in my heart,
lifting up the bones of death.

then I offer my waiting self
to the One who's never stopped
believing in me,
and the dance begins.

Joyce Rupp[2]

I cried today. It happened when I was smiling over my dry bones. At the same time I was practicing my deep breathing exercises. Suddenly I became intimately aware of a Healing Presence. I began to realize the importance of the deep journey down under, *where one can touch and be touched by the Holy One who dwells there. My tears were welcoming, holy tears. They were not tears of sadness. They were tears of deep knowing.*

Something was reborn in me, in that moment of going to the depths where Christ waited for me. My loneliness disappeared, and my tears became an eternal rain, a baptism.

In that moment I was also aware of the truth that my breathing is often too shallow. Shallow breathing can reflect a shallow life. The illusion that I am too busy to breathe deeply is a dangerous illusion.

The One who is dancing in honor of my newly revealed life keeps juggling my smiles and my tears. They are the jewels that have enlivened my dry bones. With tears in my eyes, I will continue to smile over my dry bones as the dance continues.

CHAPTER 6

Day 6—
The Dance of Conversion

Focus for the Day

Bending to moments of opportunity for conversion. It's a day for sitting by the well of daily life, open to surprise encounters.

The Fallow Season

Lean against the well and wait. This is time for soul resting.

The Sowing of the Seed

Read John 4:6–42. Stroll through this passage, lingering in its beauty.

Resting in the Soil

Allow this tiny poem to guide you to your sacred center.

> *Putting down my water jar*
> *I let myself be led*
> *to the underground rivers*
> *of my being—no buckets needed.*

The Reaping

Meditate on John 4:6–42.

1. The seed that has fallen into your soil today is a story of conversion and transformation. This Gospel woman could be you. She's thirsty. She's weary. She's fearful and cautious. She's curious. She is slowly opening to the truth. She is surprised that Jesus knows her. She's greedy for a water that will quench her thirst forever. She's amazed. And finally, she's transformed and on fire. Committed! In what way is her journey your own? Sit by the well with her today.

2. One of the touching moments in this woman's conversion story is when Jesus starts intruding in her personal life. In that instant it seems highly likely that Jesus will frighten her away. But no, she chooses to stay with the One who is slowly leading her to truth. What part of your personal life would you be most reluctant to have challenged?

3. In putting down her water jar, the woman in our story is surrendering her own plan for her life. She is making a decision to trust the direction Jesus is leading her. Name the things in your life that you need to set aside in order to be open to Jesus' dream for you? What are your water jars?

Songline

If you but knew the gift of God.

The Song of the Seed

Jesus, I saw you sitting at the well, road-weary and exhausted, but when you asked me for a drink I was startled. There was something about the tone of your voice when you said, "Give me a drink," that caught me off guard. Your voice was not demanding, as were the voices I had come to know in my life of turmoil. It seemed more as if you wanted to share a drink with me. There was a tenderness in your voice, and I felt scared. I wondered what you really wanted of me.

Then suddenly—there we were sharing living water together. I forgot about my human thirst, and I noticed that you seemed to have forgotten about your thirst also. I regret my arrogance at the moment of our meeting. Fear can do strange things to one's heart. My arrogance is gone; trust has replaced it. My desire is to drink at this well, with you, forever, as I continue the dance of life. Yet I must surrender even my dream of staying with you at the well. I hear you call me to new moments of bending and bowing to the waters of life. I leave the well knowing that your drink is making of me a wellspring of life.

May it come to pass!

Gleanings

Sitting beside the woman at the well today, I found myself reminiscing about the many people who have been instrumental in my conversion. Conversion, for me, is a great turning inside. It has always been a slow process of transformation, not something instantaneous. These turning points are very precious to me. Quite often, the catalyst for my turning points is a book I'm reading. Today my woman at the well has been Kuki Gallmann. I have been reading her book I Dreamed of Africa, *and a great softening of heart is taking place in me.[3] It has been, for me, a profound account of life and death, holy grief and pure joy. The celebration of grief and loss, the wisdom and the lessons that death and life can teach us have been my drink for today. This true story has touched my heart. There is no turning away from the great sorrow here. Neither is there a turning from the lessons that death and love can teach us. I hear the echo of my songline for today, "If you but knew the gift of God . . ." I hear Kuki speaking those same words in other ways. This book has been, for me, a turning point, a gift. It has been a drink at the well of life. It has been for me a dance of conversion.*

CHAPTER 7

Day 7—
The Dance of Sorrow

Focus for the Day

Bending to your sorrow. Integrating your sorrows into the whole of your life—seeing them as part of the good soil.

The Fallow Season

Quiet your soul. Unite your sorrows to the sorrow of Jesus, who wept over Lazarus. Let your tears water your fallow soil.

The Sowing of the Seed

Read John 11:33–44. Read this text with the ear of your heart.

Resting in the Soil

Use this little verse to help you rest in the Great Word.

> *I put away my words
> and take the time
> to savor the Word
> that gives flesh to all words.*

The Reaping

Meditate on John 11:33–44.

1. Take the tears of Jesus to your heart. Let his tears be a prayer for those who cannot weep, for those who are too fearful or too embittered to feel. Pray for a softening of the heart for anyone in your life who is unable to show tenderness.

2. Bring to your memory loved ones who have died. Name each one to God. If there is anyone you have not sufficiently grieved over, spend more time with that person. Our faith in the Communion of Saints makes it possible to receive spiritual energy from those who have died. The secret is remembering to unite with them so as to remain in communion.

3. Now try to get in touch with other sorrows in your life. Make your litany, and walk through these sorrows whatever they may be: disappointments, broken relationships, loss of health, violence done to you or to your loved ones, poverty, war, injustice. . . .

   In his sorrow Jesus said, "Take away the stone," and again, he said, "Unbind him and let him go free." Is there any sorrow in your life that is binding you, preventing you from living a joyous life?

   In union with the crucified Jesus, the martyrs of all ages, and the spirits of your own loved ones, allow the stone that keeps you in your tomb of sorrow or bitterness to be moved. Envision Jesus and your friends rolling away the stone. Hear the voice of Jesus echoing down through the years, "Unbind him; let him go free. Unbind her; let her go free!"

Songline

Take away the stone.

The Song of the Seed

The song of the seed for today will be an extension of the reaping. Let the prayer you began during meditation continue. Go for
a ceremonial walk with your sorrows. This is a time to discover
which sorrows need more of your presence. You may want to use
your rosary or Jesus beads. On each bead name a sorrow. Walk
with that sorrow until you feel ready to move to another.

Ask some prayerful questions as you walk. How has this sorrow helped me grow? What has been its hidden lesson for me? Is
there any way it has worked for my good? Or, has this sorrow
imprisoned me? Has it hardened my heart? Has it trapped me in
grief? Do I need to talk with someone about it? Is there any stone
I need to roll away in order to live life more abundantly?

A slow, meditative walk can be a beautiful prayer. Or, you
may choose to go on this walk in your imagination. As you spend
time with these sorrows, you may discover that they have become
your friends. Hidden treasures may be revealed. Or, you may find
the need to remove a stone that has kept you in bondage.

Walk with God and be at peace.

May it come to pass!

Gleanings

*Today was a tender-tough day. I feel as though I've been on
a long hike. Yet as I sit here this evening reflecting on my walks
of sorrow, I feel more peace than sorrow. It has always been a
kind of renewal and integration for me to face the things I fear.
Today I spent time with my sorrows, treating each one as a
unique friend.*

*It is easy for me to stay so busy that I don't take time to
grieve. I feed myself the lie that I will deal with my sorrows tomorrow, but tomorrow never comes. It is a kind of denial, an
escape. If I stay occupied, I suppose somehow the sorrow will*

go away, and I won't have to go through the pain of feeling what I don't want to feel. But they don't go away. They retreat deep inside me, and they are always crying for my help. Today I took my stone of denial away. I fed my sorrows the sunshine of my presence. It may take a few more walks, yet I know the day will arrive when I will be at home with my sorrows. The most helpful discovery of today has been that right in the midst of my sorrows there is always room for joy. Joy and sorrow are sisters; they live in the same house.

CHAPTER 8

Day 8—
The Dance of Joy

Focus for the Day

Bending to your joys. Have tea with your joyful soil as you begin this new day.

The Fallow Season

Rest for a few moments with your fallow soil. Practice deep breathing. Wait for the sowing.

The Sowing of the Seed

Read John 16:20–24. Invite Joy and Sorrow to stand beside you while you read.

Resting in the Soil

Just a little hint to help you put your words away.

> *What do you say*
> *when there's nothing to say?*
> *Say nothing!*

The Reaping

Meditate on John 16:20–24.

1. Happiness is elusive and fleeting. It can easily slip away. Yet underneath each moment of happiness is an eternal joy too deep to be blown away by every little wind of change. This deep joy is part of the hallowed ground of your being. A beautiful sunset or a starry night may bring you happiness. The abiding joy, however, is the reality that you are a spiritual being. You are part of a universe to which you are so intimately connected that the rhythm of its movements affects your very soul.

   A meal shared with friends may bring you happiness. The deeper joy, however, is the mystery of the bondedness that it is possible to feel within the human family. The bondedness will last long after the meal is finished and the friends are gone. Reflect on these things.

2. Having walked with your sorrows yesterday, today you contemplate your joys. Imagine the weary grown-up in you sitting with your feet in a stream. As the waters bubble over your feet, regard them as waters of joy. Your potential for joy is as great as your potential for sorrow. Yet how easy it is to go through life failing to take time to be present to individual joys! Make a list of things that bring you happiness. Beside each, write the deeper joy that cannot be taken away. Remember, happiness is fleeting; joy is eternal.

Songline

Your joy, no one can take from you.

The Song of the Seed

Jesus, deep within my heart lives a creature of joy—a little thing with wings that wants to sing through all my sorrows. It is Sorrow's sister, Joy. I have often tried to hide this joy. I've kept it buried. I've kept it a secret. But it's hard to keep secret something that sings. Can the night keep secret her stars? Or the sun hide his golden rays? Can the mountains keep secret their trees?

Help me learn the art of singing in the midst of my sorrows. Teach me to sing my way out of the tomb. Is that the secret of resurrection? Must we all learn how to come out of the tomb singing?

Jesus, you are my joy. You are the reason my joy doesn't die—even when I cry. You are the thing with wings that sings and sings and sings. You share with me your deepest emotions. My joy and sorrow are only echoes of your own passionate feelings. O Christ of the tomb, I am learning. I am learning to sing my way out of the tomb.

May it come to pass!

Gleanings

Joy and sorrow are sisters; they live in the same house. How often I've prayed for a sorrow to be lifted, a pain to be healed! Recently I've discovered that laughter can be a healing balm for well-aged grief. And a song in the midst of sadness does absolutely no harm. Sometimes when sorrows refuse to budge, I need to learn how to laugh again—how to sing again.

Today I experienced the healing qualities of joy. During my walk I tried to connect with past joys. A particularly painful time came to memory. I had made some unwise decisions about people. My belief system was in chaos, and I was feeling very alone. I realize now that because I was in such pain I simply wiped out that period of my life. Allowing myself to recall some of the joys of that era has been very healing. There is a blessing in past joys that waits for our return. Today I returned and was blessed. I have become keenly aware of the kinship of sorrow and joy.

CHAPTER 9

Day 9—
The Dance of Love

Focus for the Day

Bending and bowing to your undivided heart. There is within you a place of immense love. Dwell in that place today.

The Fallow Season

Soul resting time! Rest peacefully in your fallow soil as you begin this period of prayer. Practice deep breathing.

The Sowing of the Seed

Read Luke 7:36–50.

Resting in the Soil

Let this tiny poem lead you to your place of love.

> *Drawn to the Center*
> *by love*
> *I stay in love*
> *and leave in love.*

The Reaping

Meditate on Luke 7:36–50.

1. The nameless woman of our story had to put aside a lot of fear to come so boldly to a table where she wasn't invited. On second thought, she was invited by love. Her undivided heart invited her. Spend time in communion with this woman today. You, too, have a place of love within you that calls you to be bold. Listen to that love. What is it asking of you?

2. Call to your mind one particular sin in your life that causes you sorrow. Take that sin to your place of love and anoint it. Sorrow and love are related. Again, what is love asking of you?

Songline

Lead me to my place of love.

The Song of the Seed

Jesus, the alabaster jar of my life is being broken a little more each day. Slowly I am breaking the seal that imprisons the seeds of goodness and wisdom you have planted in me. Each day I am becoming a little more willing to anoint others with the contents of my alabaster jar: my loving-kindness, my listening heart, my understanding and mercy.

Sitting in the morning shadows in communion with you, I am reminded of the many people who have broken open the alabaster jar of their lives to anoint me. Jesus, in loving memory I name these people to you this morning. Moving through my rosary beads, I offer their names to you—one for each bead. Anoint each of these today with your loving presence. In the secret of their hearts, teach them wisdom. Make of their lives and of mine a continued dance of love.

May it come to pass!

Gleanings

The morning shadows have turned into evening shadows.
I gaze at the tall, slender vessel that sits on the shelf at my
place of prayer. It isn't translucent enough to be an alabaster
jar, yet it has helped me to focus on the life of Luke's nameless
Gospel woman, the life of Jesus, and my own life. The alabaster jar has become, for me, symbolic of a life that holds
something precious about to be poured out. As I romanced the
Word today, I envisioned the woman of our Gospel entering
the house of Simon. She is as transparent as the jar she carries.
Simon's disapproval does not daunt her or detain her. She has
heard Jesus teaching and has become a disciple.

I wonder, "Where did she first meet Jesus? When did she
become a disciple? Which words of his were the words that
changed her life? What was the good news that broke open the
alabaster jar of her heart?" We do not know when she first became a disciple, but this moment is certainly one of devoted
discipleship. Attentive to her heart, she comes boldly into
Simon's house. Her action is a kind of liturgical dance that
some folks aren't ready for. It is a moment of love gone beauti-
fully wild—an adoring gesture, falling tears, flowing hair, the
sealed jar breaking, the pouring out of costly ointment, the
anointing.

Jesus knows that the alabaster jar of her heart was broken
long before she broke the alabaster jar of ointment. He is obviously touched by her dance of love. He is being anointed as
much by the precious ointment of her faith and love as by the
contents of the jar.

As I look back through the Gospels I see clearly that the
life of Jesus has been a dance of love, a pouring out of life for
others. Perhaps he suspects he is approaching the Great Moment when the pouring out of his life will be complete. How
tender must this moment have been for him! How healing to

find a disciple who is ready to be bold about her love. How it must have pleased him to see someone who would not refuse the call to love even in the face of likely disapproval.

Each time I pour out the costly ointment of my life, there is a healthy hollowing out. A space is created in me, and Jesus rules the world from that space. There in that sacred space within, God continues to teach me wisdom. As I begin to feel at home with wisdom, I become more and more translucent.

As I continue to romance the Word of God, a great death and a great freedom will take place in me until my entire life is a majestic liturgical dance, a dance of love.

CHAPTER 10

Day 10— The Dance of Simplicity

Focus for the Day

Bending to the natural resources of your life. Dance "Simple Gifts."

The Fallow Season

Rest in your good soil. Dwell with the riches that are stored there. Wait for the Word in patience.

The Sowing of the Seed

Read Mark 6:7–13.

Resting in the Soil

Go gently into your sacred center.

> *Rest now, wait for God*
> *Take nothing on your journey*
> *You have what you need:*
> *Your poverty—God's grace.*

The Reaping

Meditate on Mark 6:7–13.

1. Authority over demons! Has it occurred to you that you have authority over the daily demons in your life? These are the things that keep you enslaved. The simplicity of your life in Christ can assist you in taking charge of these demons.

2. Only a walking stick! Jesus instructs the disciples to take nothing on their journey. This injunction suggests that they go forth believing in the simple gifts of their natural resources. Hearing and meditating on Jesus' words may help us realize that we need nothing more for our ministry than the gift of ourselves living the gospel. It isn't the props and decorations, the good films, the books and cassettes, or even the eloquent words that we might use to proclaim the gospel that are important. We are to go out in simplicity and in love. Reflect on the simplicity of your life.

3. You are asked to preach the gospel of repentance. You are to turn around and take another look at your life. Look again at what needs to be transformed. If you are willing to do this, you will be more qualified to companion others on their journeys. Look at your excess baggage. What detains and limits you? Why are you so hesitant to share the genuine gift of yourself? In his book *Free to Be Nothing,* Edward Farrell challenges us with this same concern:

> Perhaps our most hidden sin is that we have so little time for one another. We need so much more than television offers. We need to relearn how to relate eye to eye, hand to hand, heart to heart. We have to encourage one another to keep walking toward (Jesus), toward joy, toward truth. We need one another to simplify our lives and to live where God is most to be found in deeper presence with each other. We need to be purified, to be freed of excess baggage in order

to be more joyful, filled with God. Fragile people are such a revelation of God. We need to pray for our world. Our world is really hopeless. Only through Jesus' love can it be saved. What Jesus can do with a little piece of bread, He can do with us![4]

Yes, what Jesus can do with a little piece of bread He can surely do with you. Take nothing on your journey. You are the bread.

Songline

With Christ, I am enough.

The Song of the Seed

Let your prayer today be a walk. Take nothing on your journey, nothing but a walking stick. Reflect honestly on the gifts you have been given. Find strength in your natural resources as you walk. Rejoice in the truth that hidden in the center of your being is a beautiful simplicity. God wants you to discover and live that simplicity. As you walk remember the message of your theme song: "when true simplicity is found, to bend and to bow you will not be ashamed." At the end of your walk, perhaps you will be more aware that you are one of the songs the Sower is singing. With Christ, you are enough to be a healing presence to your household.

May it come to pass!

Gleanings

This songline became a special prayer today. One of the crosses that follows me through life is the haunting sense that I am never enough. When I go on a trip, I act out this painful belief by anxious fretting that I haven't packed enough. There's always something missing. When I am leading a retreat, I am often plagued with the thought that I don't have enough notes or books, or enough stories, or jokes (since I tend to be intense), enough sharing, or enough silence.

In general I find myself moving through life thinking I'm not talented enough or funny enough or intelligent enough— not good enough or beautiful enough or holy enough. Today I found myself asking, "Enough?! For whom?"

Once during a silent eight-day retreat I prayed this very simple question, "Will God ever be enough for me?" A Scripture passage with its accompanying songline found me during that retreat and has been a help in my struggle. It is the text of Philippians 4:11: "... I have learned to be content with whatever I have." Though this Word of God has not yet become a reality in my life, I often allow those words to move through me, singing up the country of my heart. Repetition is good for the soul.

I am reminded again of that text as I hear the words of Jesus, "Take nothing on your journey." As feelings of fear and resistance stir in my heart, the seed of this Word of God cracks open. I hear the song of One who believes in the good soil of my soul saying to me, You are enough! Poor, little, broken, sinful, wounded! Joyful and sorrowful! You are enough! Compassionate, idealistic, fearful! Restless, seeking, anxious! You are enough. Go simply, then, dancing the gift of yourself into my world. Take nothing on your journey. You are enough!

CHAPTER 11

Bending to the Mystery Within

The Dance of the Indwelling Presence

For ten days or more you have been keeping company with the sower and the seed. You have explored the art of bending to the Word of God and abiding in that Word. You have listened with the ear of your heart. This has been a solitary journey that you have walked *alone*. Now is the time to meet with your retreat group for sharing the fruits of your prayer and celebrating *together* the Dance of the Indwelling Presence.

Your prayer together will be enriched if you spend some time alone in prayerful preparation:

1. Before coming to the group session, meditate on the following Scripture passages: Ezekiel 37:1–14 and Colossians 1:24–29.

2. Return to the introduction and review "Suggestions for Group Prayer and Sharing."

3. Carefully read through the Prayer Service on the next pages.

4. Your needs for the first group session are as follows. The leader will attend to this. (See also "Resources" at the end of the book.)

a. Five candles

b. A Bible

c. A tape or compact disc player

d. A recording of Quaker song "Simple Gifts"

e. A recording of instrumental music of your choice

f. A recording of and/or song sheets for "Lord of the Dance"

g. Participants' own copies of *The Song of the Seed*

Group Service

A table, serving as an altar, has on it
a Bible and five unlit candles.
The candles are arranged according to the
four directions, with one candle in the center.

The leader gives any necessary directions or comments, calls for
a few moments of silence, and then reads the following:

**As these candles are lit, may we be reminded that Christ,
who is the center of our lives and the mystery within us, is
also rooted in the four corners of the earth. (Light candles.)
The four candles represent God's energizing presence in all
of creation. The center candle symbolizes the presence of
Christ in our personal lives. The Word of God for us at this
moment is**

All reply: **Christ in Us, Our Hope of Glory!**

Leader continues: **Our task is to learn how to bend and to
bow to this powerful Christ-energy within and among us.
We have gathered together to support one another in this
effort. We profess our yearning to be obedient to the Indwelling Presence. May our spirits be renewed and our dry
bones be enfleshed and refreshed as we pray the prayer of
the four winds.**

All stand.

Prayer to the Wind of the North

One person (previously appointed) holds the candle out to the north. All extend hands to the north in a gesture of receiving.

The prayer is prayed by the leader or an assigned person.

O Wind of the North, come bringing courage. Come with your power and give me the strength to endure. May I grow to appreciate your forceful breath. Take me down to the truth. Down! Down! Way down underneath my words, down there where the secrets are. Teach me to wait in the darkness without fear. If I wait long enough, someday you will breathe me up again, bringing the secrets with me. O Wind of the North, come with your courage.

Maintain a few moments of silent yearning for courage. When the person holding the candle enthrones it in a specific place in the north part of the room, this is your cue to turn to the east.

Prayer to the Wind of the East

A candle is held to the east. All extend hands to the east in a gesture of receiving.

O Wind of the East, come bringing a rebirth of hope. Come with your morning sunlight. Immerse me in the ritual of rising. Come dancing into my dry bones. Come singing songs of resurrection. O wind of the East, come with your rebirth of hope.

Allow a moment of silent yearning for a rebirth of hope. When the candle is enthroned in the east, all turn to the south.

Prayer to the Wind of the South

A candle is held to the south. All extend hands to the south in a gesture of receiving.

O Wind of the South, come bringing the energy of your love. Come singing up the country of my heart. Draw me into new possibilities for growth. Absorb me in the green journey of abundant life. Surprise me with your glory. O Wind of the South, come with the energy of your love.

Allow a moment of silent yearning for the energy of love. When the candle is enthroned in the south, all turn to the west.

Prayer to the Wind of the West

A candle is held out to the west. All extend hands to the west in a gesture of receiving.

O Wind of the West, come bringing transformation. Wrap me in mystery, and instill in me a yearning for the unknown. Caress me with your sweet breezes, and teach me to surrender. Startle me with the beauty of glorious sunsets, and give me a poet's heart. Comfort me with a death that calls me home. O Wind of the West, come with your transformation.

Allow a moment of silent longing for transformation. When the candle is enthroned in the west, all turn back to the center.

The open Bible and the remaining candle are before you.

All make a profound bow to the Word of God in the Scriptures and in one another.

Be seated and listen to the Scripture reading.

Reading and Response

Reading: Colossians 1:24–29.
Response: Free-form dance to " 'Tis a Gift to Be Simple (Simple Gifts)."

Begin the dance with joined hands, bowing to the Christ in one another, then drop hands and just move with the music, each individually using gestures that express your desire to surrender to the Mystery of Christ within you. As the music ends, form a circle again and bow to the Christ in one another.

This is the dance you were asked to use during your ten-day retreat so hopefully you will feel at home with it and it can be a joyful prayer of longing to be free.

Faith Sharing

The leader facilitates sharing, using "Guidelines for Faith Sharing" in the introduction.

Contemplative Sitting

Spend at least ten minutes in contemplative sitting. See "Guidelines for Contemplative Sitting" in the introduction.

Throughout these ten days you have practiced this prayerful way of being in silence with the Holy One. This may be your first experience of group sitting in silence. It is a profoundly healing way of being together in God.

Closing Prayer

Voice one:	Christ-in-us is the Mystery of the Word of God in all its fullness.
	To this Mystery we bow and we proclaim:
All:	Christ-in-us, our Hope of glory.
Voice two:	Christ-in-us is the Mystery hidden in ages past but now revealed to each of us.
	To this Mystery we bow and we proclaim:

All:	Christ-in-us, our Hope of glory.
Voice three:	Christ-in-us is the Mystery of a glory beyond price, a loving energy and a powerful force.
	To this Mystery, to this Energy, we bow and we proclaim:
All:	Christ-in-us, our Hope of glory.
All:	To the Christ within us, we pray. May the Mystery of your Indwelling Presence continue to fill us with your glory. Lead us in your dance of life. Help us surrender to all the new steps you wish to teach us along the way. We ask for open hearts and supple limbs that we may bend and bow to your heart's desire. We make this prayer in the name of Jesus. *May it come to pass!*

Closing Song

"Lord of the Dance," or a song of your choice.
Conclude with refreshments and fellowship.

PART II

Mending: The Feast

Take your fearful hearts
your broken relationships
your weary spirits
to the Great Mender
and celebrate
the Feast of Mending.

The focus for your next ten days is healing. The Gospels offer us many stories of recovery. People are restored in mind and body. Souls are renewed; spirits are revived. Hearts receive new courage; what is broken is mended; what is dead is brought to new life. The blind see; the lame walk. It seems that on every page of the Gospels someone is being lifted up and hope is being restored to the discouraged.

Perhaps on some days you are among the discouraged who need mending. I hope that during the days that follow, you will be led to pray about the things in your life that are broken. Because moments of healing and renewal deserve to be celebrated, I proclaim each of these healing events a feast day. I am offering you ten feast days.

My ninety-two-year-old aunt, Sister Mary John, recently told me a story that seems to fit these days of patching up our hearts. My mother was very sick when my brother Ray was little, so Ray went to live with Grandma and Grandpa Wiederkehr for almost two years. Grandma gave him a special little plate at mealtime. It had a deer on it. He loved that plate and would spend lots of time during meals playing hide-and-go-seek with the deer. He would cover up the deer with food and then scratch away the food to find the deer again. One day he dropped the plate, and it broke. He cried and cried about the broken plate. He took it to Grandpa, sobbing, "Papa, patch it, Papa patch it."

Such a tender memory—a lovely story! I don't really know the end. Did Grandpa patch it? Probably! Those were the days when people patched things instead of throwing them away. As my heart ponders my aunt's story, another image washes through my memory. I see my mother sitting by the window, the morning sunlight streaming down on her hands as she mends one of my favorite dresses. I can still see the dress—blue and pink flowers on a white background. A wind storm had literally blown me over the barbed-wire fence. I had scratched my leg badly and I had cried, not for the scratches but for the tear in the dress that I loved. After the dress was mended, I put it on and danced around the kitchen. I had not yet lost my spontaneity at that tender age; I was celebrating the feast of mending.

"Mama, mend it!" "Papa, patch it!" These are cries from the heart . . . cries from simple, loving days when our caretakers mended and patched our torn and broken treasures. For me, these are images of our Father/Mother God who is the great mender, the great caretaker. During these mending days, I trust you will be able to bring what is broken to the Divine Caretaker.

My prayer is that each day will slowly become for you a feast. At the end of the day, find some way to celebrate the feast of mending as you have experienced it. When I ask you to celebrate, I'm not suggesting anything elaborate that takes a lot of preparation. I have in mind very simple actions that could serve as a festive closing to your day. For example, you might while praying with one of your assigned Scripture texts have an insight about something that has been keeping you in bondage. Your denial is mended, and you are able to acknowledge one of your character defects. How could you close the day with a celebration of the new freedom that you feel? Here are a few suggestions:

1. In gratitude for your new freedom, brew a cup of a special blend of coffee, or prepare some other choice beverage. Light a candle at your place of prayer, and honor the breaking of those chains of denial as you sip your festive drink.

2. Listen to one of your favorite pieces of music. Dance gratefully, honoring your good soil that was receptive to the Word of God.

3. Design a greeting card describing the freedom you are feeling. Send the card to a friend sharing a little bit about your experience of healing.

These are just a few suggestions. I have no doubt that the Great Mender of broken hearts will lead you to your wells of creativity.

Before moving into your next ten days, turn back to "The Groundwork" and review "Romancing the Word."

CHAPTER I

Day 1—
The Feast of Homecoming

Focus for the Day

The mending of relationships. Coming home to God, to yourself,
to others.

The Fallow Season

Silent preparation for receiving the Word. Sit quietly, holding in
your heart whatever needs mending this day.

The Sowing of the Seed

Read Luke 15:11–33. Visualize this story as you read.

Resting in the Soil

Invite Jesus into your heart.

> *I surrender my words*
> *I abandon my thoughts*
> *Enter my heart*
> *and be at home.*

The Reaping

Meditate on Luke 15:11–33.

1. To whom do you relate in this story: the runaway son, the returning son, the father, the older brother? Write a paragraph in your journal from each person's viewpoint. You may even want to include the unmentioned mother. Stand in the shoes of each. Try to feel what each one might be feeling.

2. The son who left home returned, not because his relationship with his family was mended, but because *he was hungry.* Being hungry is a good place to start. His initial homecoming, then, was not to his family but to himself. He came home, not because he was in love, but because he had tasted his own powerlessness and realized his inability to make it on his own. How do you relate to his story? What hungers are calling you home— to God, to self, to others? How do you need to come home?

Songline

Are you hungry enough to come home?

The Song of the Seed

Jesus, deep in the good soil of my heart I hear you asking, "Are you hungry enough to come home?" It is your personal invitation to me, calling me to listen to the love that surrounds me. I have been too casual about those who love me—so slow to let them know that I care. I want to love on my own terms. When the time is right, I put out my "available" sign. The love I have taken for granted is calling me home. It is your love calling to me. It is the love of many people who care. It is my own hunger for love calling. I have spent too much time in the tents of denial. I'm ready to listen to love. I'm ready to come home.

You place a ring on my finger. You throw a cloak of mercy and love over my vagabond spirit. You have a party in my honor. You make your home in me. At this feast of homecoming I long to be the kind of home for others that you have been for me.

May it come to pass!

Gleanings

I have been walking with the prodigal son in my prayer today. I see how his journey away from home brought him face-to-face with his own powerlessness. His hunger became a grace that led him back home. That hunger worked for his good. I can identify with him as he squanders his inheritance; it is easy to see that happening in my own life. It is a spiritual inheritance that I squander. My nomadic spirit leads me into a lonely wasteland. I keep searching for something that is resting on my own doorstep. Eventually my spiritual hunger leads me back home. I am content for a while. Then, suddenly, off I go again. I have come to think of it all as a lover's struggle with God—never quite content, never believing God is at home in my heart. It is difficult for me to accept that I am loved when I'm doing ordinary things in ordinary ways and in ordinary places. Places like home!

How do I need to come home? As I reflect on that question I am drawn to a tender scene in Charles Dickens's classic Nicholas Nickleby. *Nicholas was working in a home for children that was more like a slave camp. Nicholas decided he could not stay there. He had befriended a young, crippled boy named Smike. When Smike discovered that Nicholas was leaving, he wanted to go with him. Nicholas, of course, was concerned with the reality of his poverty, his inability to offer any kind of real home to Smike. Smike, however, was not thinking of practical matters like food, clothing, and shelter. In a touching scene, he turns to Nicholas and with much passion ex-*

claims, "You are my home!"[1] *That moving scene is etched in my heart and has become a favored portrait of "home." The home that Smike sees in Nicholas is the home of a Loving Presence where he feels safe. It has little to do with walls and roofs that keep out the wind and the rain. The best home is a place in the heart where there is room for loving relationships. I yearn to be more faithful in honoring the homes God has provided for me. As I close this day by listening to Michael Card's song "I Will Bring You Home," I turn to the Mender of Hearts and pray, "You are my home."*

CHAPTER 2

Day 2—
The Feast of Healing

Focus for the Day

The mending of your reluctance to be healed. The stirring of the waters symbolizes a moment of readiness for healing.

The Fallow Season

Silent preparation for the Word. Practice deep breathing as you wait for the sowing of the seed and the stirring of the waters.

The Sowing of the Seed

Read John 5:1–9. If possible, read this text aloud.

Resting in the Soil

Let these few words lead you into the healing pool.

> *Gently falling*
> *into the pool of God,*
> *I wait patiently*
> *for the stirring of the waters.*

The Reaping

Meditate on John 5:1–9.

1. Today you are the one lying beside the pool waiting for the waters to be stirred. The stirring of the waters represents some movement of grace in your life—something that creates in you an openness for healing. It could be an insight. A retreat. A miracle on your doorstep! The beauty of nature. A conversation with a friend. A tragedy or crisis. A blessing. A book. How are the waters being stirred in your life? Be attentive to the stirring of the waters. Are you perhaps too cautious, too hesitant about claiming the grace of the moment? Does your caution and guardedness need mending?

2. When these movements of grace take place, you can be certain that the angel of God is stirring the waters in your life. This is your moment of readiness. It may also be time to talk with someone about your need for healing. Do you want to ask someone to help you to the pool? Or do you just need to accept the healing that can happen at any moment of readiness? Feast today with your moments of readiness for healing.

Songline

Be attentive to the stirring of the waters.

The Song of the Seed

O God of healing waters, you are forever stirring the waters of creation. Beholding each moment of readiness for birth, your breath touches the wound of chaos and life leaps forth. Do you remember my first feast of life when from your great watery dance one so small as I came forth? A miracle of grace emerging from your baptismal pool of creation! A part of me remembers as I proclaim, "I Am!"

And now I need a second creation. I'm lying by the pool waiting for the stirring of the waters once again, and all I ask of you, God of the Dancing Waters, is an open, unguarded heart. Take away my excuses for remaining unhealed. Take away my fear of rebirth. I don't even need to get to the pool. Bring me a cup of water to quench my thirst, to wash my face. And let me trust the one in whose flesh you choose to appear, for so often I miss the stirring of the waters—always expecting you to come some other way. Lost in a thousand excuses, I miss the moment of readiness. Today something has stirred in my heart. I want to be attentive to the stirring.

May it come to pass!

Gleanings

In my Twelve Step work, I often read books about recovery without recovering. I have a tendency to postpone serious transformation and change. I am cautious and hesitant about listening to those voices calling me to the healing pool. My prayer today has challenged me to be attentive to movements of grace in my life, the stirring of the waters *moments.*

Sometimes a wave of hope rushes through my discouraged heart just when I thought all hope was gone. A quiet joy emerges from nowhere, it seems, and stands beside a great sorrow in my soul. And there are times when feelings of love enter into places where I thought there was only disgust and intolerance. In the future I would like to be more present to those waves of hope, that quiet joy, and those feelings of love. I believe these are moments of readiness for healing. As I learn to recognize these stirrings as voices of God, I will be able to celebrate many a healing feast. Sitting beside the pool today, I have found new courage to seek healing.

CHAPTER 3

Day 3—
The Feast of Faith

Focus for the Day

The mending of your faith. Feast with the people who are models of faith for you.

The Fallow Season

Enter into the ground of your being, holding dear your faith that can help the seed grow. Spend about five minutes centering.

The Sowing of the Seed

Read Luke 5:17–26. Read carefully with your eyes of faith.

Resting in the Soil

May these few words enable you to surrender.

> *Carried by Love*
> *I enter into faith's darkness.*
> *It is a great death*
> *and a great healing.*

The Reaping

Meditate on Luke 5:17–26.

1. To be paralyzed means to be unable to move. Are there areas in your life where you feel paralyzed? What is your unique paralysis? What prevents you from moving freely?

2. If you were choosing four friends to assist you in being healed of your present-day paralysis, whom would you choose? The faith of others can be a priceless gift in your healing process. What quality in each of these friends do you most cherish? The seeds of these qualities are already in you. Water them with your faith.

Songline

Pick up your mat and go home.

The Song of the Seed

Jesus, I heard you were at home, so I came to your door, but the crowd was an immense wall that I couldn't break through. There was no room for me, so I went away to ask for help, and I found you there in the hearts of those to whom I turned. Their belief in me in the middle of my darkness has mended my faith. I move again freely, forgiven and healed. Picking up my mat, I turn toward home. O Jesus, let it be possible for honest and challenging friends to be ever in my reach!

May it come to pass!

Gleanings

One of the lines from this Scripture passage that has stayed with me is, "When Jesus saw their faith, he said, 'Your sins are forgiven.'" Their faith, not mine, but theirs . . . I spent time with those words today remembering how the faith of others has hastened my healing. All this musing led me to reflect gratefully on the value of spiritual friendship. I prayed for the four people I asked to bring me to Jesus. Now before the day ends I want to write a note of thanks to each person. Their faith has often enabled me to pick up my mat and go home.

CHAPTER 4

Day 4—
The Feast of Leisure

Focus for the Day

The mending of your busyness. Focus on ways to restore your contemplative spirit.

The Fallow Season

Surrender your thoughts. Quiet your soul. Lean back into God and wait.

The Sowing of the Seed

Read Luke 10:38–42.

Resting in the Soil

You are being led to the quiet room of your heart.

> *Like Mary in love*
> *I sit at your feet,*
> *Surrendering all plans*
> *The work can wait.*

The Reaping

Meditate on Luke 10:38–42.

1. In honor of Mary, spend more time in the chapel of your heart today. Then find someone at whose feet you can sit. Listen to someone else's wisdom. Give yourself the gift of being attentive to the voice of God speaking to you through everyone and everything you meet this day.

2. In honor of Martha, find some task to do joyfully, without complaining. That means leisurely! Let your day be a feast of leisure. Choose some specific work, and try to do it more contemplatively. Creative doing flows out of loving being.

3. Let this descriptive passage of an old woman having tea minister to both the Martha and the Mary in you.

   My kitchen linoleum is so black and shiny that I waltz while I wait for the kettle to boil. This pleasure is for the old who live alone. The others must vanish into their expected roles.[2]

   Do not vanish into your expected role today. What extravagance will you lavish on yourself today on this Feast of Leisure?

Songline

Quietly, joyfully, gratefully, without complaining!

The Song of the Seed

O Loving Being! O Playful Creator! Love your way into the depths of my being today so that whatever I do will be a prayer, whether it be making bread or boiling water, visiting the sick or mowing the grass, taking a walk or teaching a class, having a picnic or comforting the sorrowful. May it all be an act of love and a feast of leisure. In all that I do, may I remember that I am a tabernacle of the Holy Mystery, a place where you dwell. May my moments of quiet listening at your feet lead me out again into the market-place joyfully, gratefully, without complaining.

May it come to pass!

Gleanings

As the stars again become visible tonight, I am reminded of a feast of leisure from my childhood days. I remember, on sum-mer evenings, sitting outside on a quilt with Mama waiting for the stars to come out. Looking back at that moment with my adult eyes, I understand that God is Someone who has taken the time to sit on a quilt with me waiting for beauty. She is a Mother of Presence. I need only invite her into my moments of leisure. Her presence will empower my presence.

As I tried to bring a deeper quality of presence to all my works this day, I found God moving through the day with me, like a Mother, opening my eyes to beauty. Quietly, joyfully, gratefully, without complaining, I welcomed all the beauty that crossed my path.

CHAPTER 5

Day 5—
The Feast of
the Awakened Child

Focus for the Day

The mending of all within you that has grown too old, too serious, too sleepy. It's a day for waking up the child.

The Fallow Season

Be grateful that God has touched down in your fallow soil. Bask in the Presence for about five minutes.

The Sowing of the Seed

Read Mark 5:21–24, 35–43.

Resting in the Soil

Enter the chapel of your soul with these words on your lips.

> *I cannot hurry into holiness*
> *I put my head in my heart.*
> *in wordless loving*
> *I will let You have me.*

The Reaping

Meditate on Mark 5:21–24, 35–43.

1. In this story Jesus does not come immediately to heal the child when the father asks. He attends to someone else first and then goes to the child when it appears to be too late. Reflect on moments in your life when something in you died and God seemed to arrive too late. To whom do you turn in such moments? Does God ever arrive too late?

2. Pray with your inner child today. Look underneath the age you are, and allow yourself to have a glimpse of some of those other ages. Is there any age you need to be today? Does your three-, seven-, or eleven-year-old child have something to say to you?
   Ponder these words from the storyteller Sandra Cisneros:

   > What they don't understand about birthdays and what they never tell you is that when you're eleven, you're also ten, and nine, and eight, and seven, and six, and five, and four, and three, and two, and one. . . . Like some days you might say something stupid, and that's the part of you that's still ten. Or maybe some days you might need to sit on your mama's lap because you're scared, and that's the part of you that's five. And maybe one day when you're all grown up maybe you will need to cry like if you're three, and that's okay. That's what I tell Mama when she's sad and needs to cry. Maybe she's feeling three.[3]

3. What you need is trust. Take these words of Jesus to your heart. God wants to take your hand and raise you from whatever sleep is preventing you from living with an awakened heart. Can you trust that hand? After raising the sleeping child, Jesus said, "Give her something to eat." Make plans to feed your awakened child. How will you do this?

Songline

Fear is useless; what is needed is trust.

The Song of the Seed

Suddenly I am a child again
Awakening from a deep sleep,
trusting a hand
held out in the darkness
inviting me to rise and live.

Suddenly I am a child again
Allowing eternal questions
to rise in my soul,
asking the questions aloud, aloud
in silence, in silence, in silence
and finally a silence that is loud.
No longer afraid
to seek the mystery, questioning
No longer afraid of eternal questions.

Suddenly I am not afraid of what I do not know
Unafraid of what I do not understand
Suddenly I am delighted
to take the hand of an unseen God,
leading me through a comforting darkness
in which I do not see the stars
but feel them rising in my heart.

Suddenly I am a child
unashamed and unafraid
to reach out in the darkness for a hand.

Suddenly I am an awakened child.

Gleanings

In the story of Jesus awakening the twelve-year-old girl I am so moved by his request to the parents to give her something to eat. He didn't say, "Thank God for her healing," or "Go and sin no more." No! He simply said, "Feed her!"

As I prayed with the awakening child in me today, I decided to spend some time feeding her. I fed myself with some of the things for which I have been starving: fresh air, wind and rain, green trees and bird song. I spent time outside with nature. I walked in the rain. Many healing, rainy memories from my past returned. It was all part of the feeding process. This evening I feel I've lost a few pounds of heaviness of spirit and gained some lightness of heart. As I move into this good night and into sleep again, I continue to hear Jesus' voice saying, "Feed her!" I hope I will remember that voice and advice in the morning. It is a voice I would like to trust and advice I want to follow.

CHAPTER 6

Day 6—
The Feast of Freedom

Focus for the Day

The mending of your self-made prisons. Pray about the things that keep you in bondage.

The Fallow Season

Make an intention to place yourself in God's hands. Move into the prayer of quiet.

The Sowing of the Seed

Read Mark 5:1–20.

Resting in the Soil

Let this short prayer lead you to your sacred center.

> *O Ancient Love*
> *Take from me everything*
> *except my poverty*
> *and your grace.*

The Reaping

Meditate on Mark 5:1–20.

1. The man who lived among the tombs lived in the area of the Gerasenes, also known as Gadarenes. The word means walled in or fortified. Is there any area of your life where you are so walled in or bound by chains that you need the touch of Jesus or a disciple of Jesus to bring you back to your senses? How do you live among the tombs? How would you like to be freed?

2. Can you recall times in your life when you have longed for freedom and yet resisted it? If so, pray about your resistance.

3. There is no need to live among the tombs. Spend time today attending the deep resources of life within you. These are all part of your good soil.

Songline

> *Life, without chains.*

The Song of the Seed

Jesus, friend of those who live among the tombs, this gospel sounds familiar. I've been there in those stony, walled-up places, bound with chains, imprisoned by my words and opinions. I lived among tombs of my own making until the day you walked into my tombs and cut the chains that kept me in the darkness. Years of walls and months of masks fell crumbling in your presence. You called me by my name and led me to my own good soil. I celebrate the day you walked among my tombs giving me a taste of freedom. And though I have days when the tomb still wants its way, something in the depths of me keeps calling me to freedom.

> *May it come to pass!*

Gleanings

As I glean through this day of walking among the tombs, I am drawn to pray about Step Six of the Twelve Steps of A.A. Step 6 suggests that I am entirely ready *to have God remove all my defects of character. For a long time now, I've been working on this step. I get choked on those two little words,* entirely ready. *Sitting among my tombs today, I thought about my unending resistance to deep spiritual growth. Instead of beating myself for my neglect, I've decided to pray a prayer of affirmation.*

Here is my prayer:

I am entirely ready to have the chains that keep me bound be broken. I am entirely ready for the walls I've built around myself to be torn down. I am entirely ready to give up my need to be in control of every situation. I am entirely ready to let go of my resentments. I am entirely ready to grow up. I am entirely ready to give up my unhealthy attachments. I am entirely ready to stop living among the tombs.

Even as I say these words I feel my resistance. I also feel the blessing of my yearning for the words I say to come true in my life. I prayed today as if I were entirely ready, and somehow in the midst of my prayer Jesus came walking among my tombs, as he has done so many times before. So once again I celebrated the feast of freedom. And I remembered other days, other chains, other tombs, and other feasts. Every time I bring these things to prayer, I feel a little more ready to let go. Perhaps some day the feast will turn into a solemnity.

CHAPTER 7

Day 7—
The Feast of Seeing Clearly

Focus for the Day

The mending of your blindness.

The Fallow Season

It is time for quieting your soul. (Take about five minutes.)

The Sowing of the Seed

Read Mark 8:22–26. May the good soil in you enjoy this Word of God.

Resting in the Soil

You are being led into the heart of God.

> *Touch me deeply*
> *while I rest in You*
> *that when I awake*
> *I may see Your face.*

The Reaping

Meditate on Mark 8:22–26. Gather insights and pray your questions.

1. Who are the people in your life who have brought you to new vision? Invite them to accompany you on your journey. Draw strength from their strength. These may be members of your own household of faith, or you may have met them in films, books, or the newspaper.
2. In what areas of your life do you long for a second touch? Envision Jesus taking you by the hand and leading you.

Songline

I need a second touch.

The Song of the Seed

Jesus, sometimes my eyes seem as tightly closed as those of a newborn kitten, and I need a hand, your hand, to lead me down the healing road to help me see more clearly. I need a second touch. But spittle, Jesus? I don't know! So earthy, crude, and unacceptable! I thought perhaps you would enfold me and hold me to your heart, a gentle anointing restoring all lost sight! Are you sure a seed of healing fell into my soil? Or is my resistance to grace stifling my song? I want to be healed of my limited vision. I want to see more clearly. And though I'd like to tell you how to heal me, I ask instead for the grace to accept your second touch however it may come. I need a second touch. Jesus, touch me one more time.

May it come to pass!

Gleanings

Silence, now! The house is quiet. I've thought a lot about that second touch today. How picky I can be about how grace

comes to me, how I am healed, and who is involved in the
healing process! There are opportunities for second touches all
over the place. I reject a lot of second touches.

Jesus touched the blind man's eyes with spittle. That
doesn't seem very appropriate to me. As I was out walking
today, praying my songline and singing up the country of my
heart, the story of Naaman the leper came to my memory
(2 Kings 5:1–27).

I am a lot like Naaman. He wasn't very happy with the
command to go wash in the river Jordan seven times. He
stormed away from the prophet. He wanted a better river to
wash in than the dirty Jordan. He thought his healing would
take place in loftier ways: a gentle laying on of hands, perhaps.
As I reflect on this second touch that I long for today, I understand that the mending of my blindness comes in unexpected
ways. Often it is a song on the radio instead of a sermon in
church. Sometimes the evening news startles my compassionate
heart out of its lethargy. There are times when healing is offered to me through a person I don't even respect. A curtain
goes up suddenly, and I'm able to see that person in an entirely
new light. Today I prayed with memories of healings that came
to me in unexpected ways.

CHAPTER 8

Day 8—
The Feast of
Encouragement

Focus for the Day

The mending of your fears and discouragement through the discovery of Jesus alive and in your midst.

The Fallow Season

Quiet your spirit at the beginning of this day, and wait for God to enter into your depths. Be attentive to your breathing.

The Sowing of the Seed

Read Matthew 28:1–12. Move slowly through this text with an open, listening heart.

Resting in the Soil

Let God's angel lead you into the tomb.

> *Descending into the tomb*
> *of my discouragement,*

I wait patiently
for the stone to be rolled away.

The Reaping

Meditate on Matthew 28:1–12. Open your heart to new insights.
Pray your questions.

1. Sometimes there are places in our lives that resemble the tomb
   experience of these women. Life seems absent. Sadness akin to
   fear takes over. Are you in such a place now? How do you need
   life returned? Do you need encouragement at the tomb? Do
   you know someone else who is in a discouraging place? Make
   plans to spend time at your own tomb or the tomb of another.

2. Let the sunrise of the light of Christ shine on all of your discouragements. Let your prayer be a childlike seeking of Jesus
   through all the hours of this day. As you awaken to the stirring of life in unexpected places, celebrate the little resurrections you discover.

Songline

Do not be afraid; life is stirring within you.

The Song of the Seed

Jesus, I have been entombed in my many discouragements. I have
forgotten the life force within and around me. I want to walk
through this day with the angel of resurrection. Her bright wings
surround me! She brings good news of the presence of Jesus to
all my dark places. How strange to live in darkness and discouragement with life so close at hand! I give you my fear and my

sadness. It is time to allow the angel at the tomb of my heart to restore my joy and awareness of life.

May it come to pass!

Gleanings

I can only imagine the joy that replaced the discouragement in the hearts of the women at the tomb when suddenly Jesus stood before them, alive. It had to be a Feast of Encouragement! Today I celebrated many such feasts. There have been countless little resurrections in my personal life. I have a tendency to discount the little resurrections in favor of the big ones. Yet in some way all those little resurrections are Easter moments worthy of recognition.

I go through very dry periods in my faith life when Jesus seems as good as dead. How encouraging, then, when somehow in the midst of all the dry wood of my life, the green starts showing through. Jesus starts making sense again. There is suddenly room in my heart for a love I thought I had lost. When this happens, no matter what day of the week, it's time to have a Sunday, an Easter, a Feast of Encouragement. In many ways I have abandoned Sunday as the traditional Christian feast day. I allow it to become just another day. To correct that sad neglect, I would like to practice having a short Sunday anytime I feel the life stirring again. From this day forward, when I experience Jesus' return after a dry spell, it will be, for me, a Feast of Encouragement.

CHAPTER 9

Day 9—
The Feast of
God as a Refuge

Focus for the Day

The mending of the storms of your life.

The Fallow Season

Take refuge in God. Let your heart be still.

The Sowing of the Seed

Read Psalm 107. If possible, read the psalm aloud.

Resting in the Soil

Let these words entice you into the heart of God.

> *In the restless*
> *stormy waters of my being*
> *I put my head in my heart*
> *and listen to your heartbeat.*

The Reaping

Meditate on Psalm 107.

1. This psalm offers several images of turbulence you may have experienced:

   a. Wandering in the wilderness lost and hungry, verses 4–5

   b. Being imprisoned in chains of your own making, the result of having rebelled against God's Word, verses 10–12

   c. Feeling sick and troubled because of your sins, verses 17–20

   Look at each of these in relation to your personal history. Pray with your own unique storm.

2. In this psalm the answer to each stormy moment is a moment of finding refuge and shelter in God. Turn to God in each of your personal storms. How do you allow God to be your refuge?

3. On your spiritual voyage, remember that the *deep waters* symbolize the unconscious. Spend time practicing contemplation in the deep waters of your underworld today. It is here you will be able to experience God as your refuge. Meditate on this advice given to us by an anonymous teacher from the early twentieth century:

   . . . in turbulent times . . . sink down three fathoms below the storm, where the stillness is; here where all things are accomplished, the quiet where all things are done. When you come to the surface you will bring some of this calm, this undisturbed peace with you; and the more you do this under stress, the more involuntary it will become so that eventually your mind will first seek the divine instead of human wisdom.[4]

Songline

You are my refuge in the storms of life.

The Song of the Seed

Jesus, once on the sea of Galilee you calmed a storm to put the hearts of those you loved at rest. There are so many storms sweeping across our land today: storms of war and violence, confusion and sin, sorrow and despair, greed and poverty. Put out your hand again. Teach us how to trust in you as our refuge.

Bring our ships in over the stormy seas of wrong decision, addictive behavior, and broken dreams. Bring our ships in to the harbor of the safety of your heart. I pray, not for a safety that is free from the waters of challenge and risk, but for a safety full of trust and hope in the shelter of your presence.

May it come to pass!

If you have access to Rory Cooney's cassette tape *Safety Harbor,* use the song "Safety Harbor" for your prayer. (See "Resources.")

Gleanings

The image of wandering in the wilderness lost and hungry struck a chord in me today. There is a restlessness that has plagued me all my life. It is that hungry, lost part of me pacing within and always looking for home. It feels like being lost in my own heart.

There is a wild place within me where untamed creatures seem to dwell. Yet I am discovering that alongside those untamed things lives something tame and completely at ease with the wild things. When my restlessness subsides, I get a glimpse of its face. It is a kind of gentleness and understanding that is at home with the wild things. When I am at peace with this beautiful wildness, I feel closest to God. My restlessness comes from my inability to accept the blessing of the paradox of the marriage of the wild and tame creature within. No wonder I feel lost and hungry, living in all the confusion that comes from fighting! The storm comes in the fighting. The peace comes in abiding. So I will learn to abide and be at home with who I am. For I have come to believe that this wild-tame creature inside me is a part of God.

CHAPTER 10

Day 10—
The Feast of Your Identity

Focus for the Day

The mending of your denials.

The Fallow Season

Entrust yourself to God's hands. Breathe in the truth of who you really are. Breathe out all denial.

The Sowing of the Seed

Read Luke 22:54–62. As you read, imagine that you are Peter. You are cautious and following at a distance.

Resting in the Soil

Let Jesus lead you into the fire of his heart.

> *Sitting at the charcoal fire*
> *in your heart*
> *I am warmed*
> *by your forgiveness.*

The Reaping

Meditate on Luke 22:54–62. Open your heart to the insights and challenge of this text.

1. Verse 54 suggests that Peter was cautious and followed at a distance. This is an identity crisis for Peter. He seems unsure of who he is in relation to Jesus. He is afraid. Can you identify with Peter in this scene? What is your experience of *following at a distance?*

2. Peter sat among them, but he was not really one of them. Even though he denied that he knew Jesus, the river of tears within him would soon tell the truth. Are there subtle ways that you deny your relationship with Jesus? How are you tempted to just be one of the crowd at the charcoal fires of your life?

3. Denial of any kind is a barrier to one's true self. Carefully and lovingly ask yourself this question: Is there a place in my life where I live in denial? Invite your tears to wash away your denials that you may be able to celebrate the feast of your true identity.

Songline

Free me from living in denial.

The Song of the Seed

Jesus, I'm tired of following you at a distance. I long to be there in the heart of things, standing in the crowd unafraid to live out my relationship with you. Today I want to celebrate the feast of who I really am, in You. I hold dear my identity as an extension of your love. I want to be true to that identity.

Guide me to the discovery of my true self. When I deny my gifts, I deny you, because you are the giver of those gifts. When

I deny my weaknesses, I refuse the joy that can come from self-disclosure. Teach me to allow both my weaknesses and my strengths to work for my good.

May it come to pass!

Gleanings

Denial is like a boulder hanging around my neck, a wall that blocks out the sunlight. Sometimes it's like a prison preventing me from moving freely, or like a loneliness that keeps me forever homeless. I wonder why so many of us insist on living in denial. And I wonder about the causes of denial. Pride, shame, and fear are some of the root causes that come to mind.

Much of my denial comes from fear. My major denial centers around my refusal to trust the God who wants to companion me. And so, like Peter, I follow at a distance. Deep in this frightened old heart of mine, I know if I follow more closely there are things in my life I'll have to change. When I do not trust, I do not allow myself to be nurtured and healed. I do not allow myself to be a channel for the divine life. God uses me for a channel anyway, but it would be so much more delightful if I could live awake to what is happening in this divine exchange.

Whatever form denial takes, it always imprisons me in some way. I deny I have a specific addiction, and so I am unable to use the grace of confession to help me on the road to recovery. I deny I am afraid of failure, and so I am not able to dialogue honestly with that fear. I deny I am jealous or resentful, so the freedom that comes from self-disclosure never blossoms.

Denial is always a way of following at a distance. My reflection today keeps calling me to the truth that can be found in living at the center.

CHAPTER 11

Mending Your Reluctance to Own the Mystery Within

The Feast of the Indwelling Presence

For the past ten days you have been honoring your need for healing. You have celebrated a Feast of Mending each day. Now once again you are preparing to meet with your spiritual family to share the Song of the Seed together.

1. Before coming to the group prayer session, spend some time reflecting on the following Scripture passages: John 20:24–29 and Genesis 28:10–22.

2. Spend a little time reading through the prayers on the following pages.

3. Bring a stone with you to the prayer session.

4. You may wish to return to the introduction and review "Suggestions for Group Prayer and Sharing."

5. The leader will assign three readers for the Prayer Service and make sure the items in the following list are available. (See also "Resources.")

   a. A Bible

   b. A candle

   c. A stone for each participant

  d. A table with a small dish of oil (any kind of vegetable oil will be fine)

  e. A large flat stone or a slab of wood to serve as a platform to lay stones upon

  f. A tape or compact disc player

  g. A recording of and/or song sheets for "Holy Darkness"

  h. A recording of instrumental music of your choice

  i. A recording of and/or song sheets for the Quaker song "How Can I Keep from Singing?"

Group Service

Your *sacred space* includes
a table with Bible enthroned, a candle,
and a small dish of oil for anointing stones.

Guided Meditation

During the opening meditation, participants are asked to hold the stones they brought in the palms of their hands.

  Leader reads slowly, pausing at appropriate times:

Sometimes it is difficult to celebrate the Feast of the In-dwelling Presence. We may be experiencing instead what feels like an indwelling absence. We bring to this prayer all those things that make it difficult to own the Mystery within: our fear, darkness, doubt, discouragement, confusion, brokenness, sorrow, regret. We bring our lost hopes and dreams.

We come wondering and questioning. Is it possible for the dark days of our lives to be changed into prayer even now? Is it reasonable to suppose that we can learn to sing in the midst of the darkness? How is it possible for the darkness

to be called *holy darkness?* Is it conceivable that our
doubts could become our blessings?

Are we willing to take a new look at those places in our
lives where God once seemed absent? Will we be able to
stand before these places with new eyes and cry out,
"Truly Yahweh was in this place and I never knew it"
(Gen. 28:16). And finally, are we ready to anoint these
stony places of our lives, allowing them to be changed into
bread for our nourishment? Are we ready for our doubts
to become blessings? Are we open to see how God visits us
in the darkness?

Sit quietly now with those dark, doubting places of your
life. Yearn to understand how God visits you even here. As
you clutch your stone, pray to discover a hidden grace in
every darkness that it may truly be a holy darkness.

Maintain a few moments of silence. Sing "Holy Darkness"
or a song of your choice.

Opening Prayer

All: O Christ of the lonely times.
                  Be with us in all our dark, doubting moments
                  when, like Thomas, we want to put a finger
                  into your wounded side to be certain
                  you've truly risen in our lives.
                  Change our darkness into holy darkness.
                  In the name of Jesus we pray.

Reading: John 20:24–29.

Faith Sharing

Share some of your "Thomas moments" with one another. Leader
or assigned person facilitates sharing.

When is it difficult for you to experience the Mystery of Christ within? Why is it so hard to believe in the Indwelling Presence? How healthy is the risen Jesus in your life? Please note: we need never be ashamed of our seasons of doubt. These doubts can deepen our faith, thus becoming blessings in disguise.

Do you have any blessings or insights from the past ten days of your retreat that you want to share with the group?

Contemplative Sitting

After a period of sharing, the leader invites the group into ten or fifteen minutes of a quiet, prayerful way of being with God together in silence. See "Guidelines for Contemplative Sitting" in the introduction.

Our reading from Genesis is a preparation for our next exercise, reclaiming the lost prayers of our lives.

Reading and Response

Reading: Genesis 28:10–22.

Leader: There is a gift hidden away in the frail envelope of your being. It is the gift of your brokenness. The mysterious thing about this gift is that God's presence isn't experienced immediately. Sometimes it takes a backward glance: Jacob after his dream cries out, "Truly Yahweh was in this place and I never knew it." Let those words move through your heart now as you stand before life experiences in which the Indwelling Presence of God was not felt—those places where you could not feast because the darkness did not appear to be holy darkness.

In the following ritual you are asked to make Jacob's prayer your own. As you hold your stone in your hand, we will name some of those dark places.

Let us all respond together.

All: Truly Yahweh was in this place and I never knew it.

Voice one: I remember a season of blindness. It was difficult to see the truth. My opinions were always the best. I had to be in control. The gift of others couldn't reach me, because I had built my walls too high. I dared anyone, even God, to look over those walls and really *see* me. Yet all the while I was crying to be known. And even in that dark place . . .

All: Truly Yahweh was in this place and I never knew it.

Voice two: There was once a Gethsemane in my life, a great sorrow that crowded out my joy. No matter which way I turned, darkness engulfed me. My grief was like a mountain that hid all of heaven from me. But even then . . .

All: Truly Yahweh was in this place and I never knew it.

Voice one: There was once a deep resentment in my life. Violence had been done to me, and forgiveness seemed out of the question. I wore my animosity like a cloak. I clutched it to my heart and wouldn't let it go. I tried to remember the Indwelling Presence to no avail. My angry, unforgiving spirit was all I could taste. And even there . . .

All: Truly Yahweh was in this place and I never knew it.

Voice two: There was a place and time in my life when I was smothered by addictive behavior, pouring my life's energy into things from which I longed to be free—wrestling with the powers of darkness, limping away from the struggle without experiencing the blessing. Yet in the midst of it all . . .

All: Truly Yahweh was in this place and I never knew it.

Voice one: There was once a room of fear in my life. It was a dark room that crowded out all my love. It distracted me from the Indwelling Presence and stifled my joy and my hope. It was a place of doubt and confusion. I was searching desperately to find peace but willing to trust no one. It was a time of defensiveness, loneliness, despair. And even there . . .

All: Truly Yahweh was in this place and I never knew it.

Voice two: And now, in silence, let us name any personal darkness we wish to bring to this prayer. (Moment of silence.) As we stand in these places, in faith, we cry out . . .

All: Truly Yahweh was in this place and I never knew it.

Ritualization of These Dark Moments

Leader: We ritualize God's presence in our lives during these dark times by coming forward and anointing our stone with oil.

Participants use oil to trace a sign of the cross on the stone, heaping the stones on the altar table as a memorial of God's visitation. During this time you may wish to play some soft music as you silently pray for one another.

Closing Prayer

Leader: **O Ancient Love,**

We honor the Mystery of Christ's presence in us. We celebrate the feast of this Indwelling Presence. We have changed this room into a House of Bread, another Bethel. You are here in ways we did not know. We cherish your presence. We receive your joy in the midst of our sorrows. We receive your love in the midst of our fears. We receive your light in the midst of our darkness. We receive your song in our hearts and so we sing. How can we keep from singing?

Closing Song

"How Can I Keep from Singing?"
Conclude with refreshments and fellowship.

PART III

Tending: The Gift

Deep within your soul
there is a *knowing place*
a sanctuary where gifts are nurtured.
Enter that sacred space.
Spend time there tending your gifts.
There in the chapel of your heart
you will become a gift to be given.

"The gift you have received, give as a gift" (Matt. 10:8, NAB). In these last days of your retreat, I encourage you to tend the gift you have received that you may be able to give it as a gift to build up the Body of Christ.

How do you cultivate your gifts? What do you do to nurture the gifts with which you have been blessed? Gifts need to be awakened, developed, and affirmed. As you tend a garden, so too you must tend each gift.

In her book on creativity and addiction, Linda Schierse Leonard has this to say about tending the gift within:

> Both the receiving of the gift and the work to polish the jewel and pass it on to others require sacrifice—one must offer oneself up as an open channel. The energy behind such a sacrifice comes from our spiritual longing. If we divert that longing through addictions . . . we lose access to the creative.[1]

There is a priestly power in each gift that is part of our inheritance. Sometimes I forget to nurture my gifts, and so I live without the help of that special power. These words from an ancient collection of Christian writings encourage me: "Failure to do the good that is within your power is hard to forgive; but mercy and prayer reclaim the negligent."[2]

Let these next ten days be days of mercy and prayer. Have mercy on your negligent self. As your remembrance of these gifts replaces your forgetfulness, you will find new ways to tend them rather than ignore or doubt them.

Deep within each person there is *a knowing place*. In the days that follow, I will be inviting you to enter into that place. Spend time there: waiting and loving, trusting, remembering, discovering, and tending the gift you've been given, the gift that you are. I want to share with you two memories of being led to my own knowing place.

The first memory comes from my childhood. God gave me the gift of exuberance for life. But one day my exuberance died.

It died on the day my little sister died. Then one day it slowly began to return. It happened like this: I was sitting by my favorite pine tree. I was tired of feeling sad. Off in the distance, I saw the cows in the barnyard. One of them was licking the salt block. That image, still vivid in my memory, fed my sadness, for it reminded me of when Dorothy and I used to sneak up to the salt block and lick it with the cows (sounds appalling now). Gazing out toward the barnyard, I suddenly felt drawn to walk through it and on to the meadow. The meadow had been our favorite place to play. We danced there, pretending we were on stage. I had not been back since she died. When I reached the meadow, I sat down in the tall grasses and cried.

It was early September. There was a warm wind blowing, and the grasses were swaying in the wind. Suddenly something was different. It was as though Dorothy was inside me. I felt her calling me. She was moving me to my feet, and suddenly I was dancing again. I got up and danced with the grasses and wildflowers. I kept crying, but at least I was dancing. After that I went there often, until finally I could dance without crying. I feel very tender as I tell this story, and some lines from one of Marge Piercy's poems make me smile:

> My garden's a chapel, but a meadow
> gone wild in grass and flowers
> is a cathedral.[3]

I still carry my meadow cathedral with me. It is part of my knowing place.

My second memory of returning to a knowing place is very much a part of my present life. It is a moment that I share with my sisters in community. A profoundly simple, yet lovely, monastic ritual that we practice is called *statio*. *Statio* is a Latin word meaning "a standing together." On Sundays and solemnities, we stand together outside the chapel before vespers. This is a silent moment of preparation before our communal prayer. It is easy to forget who we are and what we are about to do, so we stand together to remember who we are. It is a time of purification of mind and heart. As we stand we try to let go of resentments, anxieties, distractions. We tend the gifts of love, reverence, and simplicity so that we may attend our evening prayer with pure hearts. We go to our knowing place and wait.

As we process into chapel, we stand before the sacred space of the sanctuary and bow to the holy of holies; then turning to our partner we offer a deep bow of recognition. That person, too, is holy.

I hope these next days will be rich and fruitful ones as you tend some of the gifts God has given you. Before moving into this last ten days, turn back to "The Groundwork" and once again review "Romancing the Word."

CHAPTER I

Day 1—
The Gift of Discipleship

Focus for the Day

Tending God's call. A renewal of your call to discipleship.

The Fallow Season

Quieten your soul. It is time for wordless communion with God.

The Sowing of the Seed

Read Mark 1:14–22. Open your heart as you move through this text. Listen intently.

Resting in the Soil

Let this little poem lead you into the great silence.

> *Abandoning the nets*
> *of my thoughts and words,*
> *I follow you willingly*
> *into the great silence.*

The Reaping

Meditate on Mark 1:14–22. Romance the Word. Gather insights. Pray your questions.

1. Repent and believe the good news. The reign of God is near. Abandon anything that hides the reign of God from you. To repent means to take a discerning look at your life. Look at your nets: the net of your busyness, the net of your forgetfulness, the net of your possessions, the net of your self-centeredness, the net of your control, and so on. Go to your knowing place and repent. Listen deeply. Which nets do you need to abandon to free the reluctant disciple in you?

2. The phrase "they immediately abandoned their nets" is a bit jarring. How do we become integrated and centered enough to abandon what we need to abandon? How shall we awaken the sleeping disciple within?

3. William Johnston may have the answer to becoming a disciple in these very wise words:

> You must remember that unless you renounce everything you possess you cannot be the disciple of Jesus. This is the contemplative process. Slowly, ever so slowly, projections and masks and fears and anxieties and addictions fall away.
>
> The little foxes die or scamper off into the dark night. Let them go. Let everything go. And you become your true self.
>
> And as you let go, there arises from the centre of your being the blind stirring of love, the living flame of love, the divine fire. This is a pure gift of God: it is nothing other than the indwelling Holy Spirit.[4]

As we yield to the Indwelling Presence, our human wisdom is integrated with divine wisdom. It happens slowly. There is wisdom in the word *slowly*. The disciple in each of us is awakened slowly. It is love that awakens the disciple. The fire of love burns away the ego, and we are filled with gratitude. Reflect on these things.

Songline

Slowly . . .

The Song of the Seed

Life unfolds
a petal at a time
slowly.

The beauty of the process is crippled
when I try to hurry growth.
Life has its inner rhythm
which must be respected.
It cannot be rushed or hurried.

Like daylight stepping out of darkness,
like morning creeping out of night
life unfolds slowly
a petal at a time
like a flower opening to the sun,
slowly.

God's call unfolds
a Word at a time
slowly.

A disciple is not made in a hurry.
Slowly I become like the One
to whom I am listening.

Life unfolds
a petal at a time
like you and I
becoming followers of Jesus,
discipled into a new way of living
deeply *and* slowly.

Be patient with life's unfolding petals.
If you hurry the bud it withers.
If you hurry life it limps.
Each unfolding is a teaching
a movement of grace
filled with silent pauses
breathtaking beauty
tears and heartaches.

Life unfolds
a petal at a time
deeply *and* slowly.

May it come to pass!

Gleanings

A small word followed me through the day! Slowly—*just one little word. It came as a surprise. My Songline turned into a songword, slowly . . .*

I do nothing slowly. I was born with speed in my feet. I am driven. I was so sure that my word for today was immediately. The net of my restlessness has been catching nothing but unrest. I knew it had to be surrendered at once. After all, the apostles left everything and followed Jesus immediately. Surely I should do the same. But wait a minute! Immediately sounds like a word from a threatening parent. Maybe the disciples left everything to follow Jesus not out of obedience to a call but because of the excitement of it all. This young, charismatic itinerant preacher touched their venturesome spirits. Following him was more exciting than mending nets, waiting for bites, and cleaning fish. So the apostles may have gone off with Jesus not quite sure about their motives.

But then, of course, later they got hooked. They found themselves caught by love, reverence, and friendship for this *earthy man who seemed to know heaven so well. God had been pretty much of a hidden God for them. Jesus made this God seem close. They were drawn by love, and they started following—not so immediately perhaps, but ever so slowly.*

I was surprised when the word slowly *came to me. I had already chosen the word* immediately *for my songline after my first reading of the Scripture. It challenged me. It suggested that I put aside all obstacles to discipleship and that I do it quickly.*

But when I came out of the great silence, I heard a faint song. It was way down there in my good soil singing up the country of my heart. Even as my lips formed the word immediately, *One from within kept whispering, "slowly."*

Finally the songline reached me, slowly . . .

CHAPTER 2

Day 2—
The Gift of the
Bread of Your Life

Focus for the Day

Tending your nurturing qualities. You are bread, broken and given.

The Fallow Season

Enter into stillness. No words—just a naked yearning for God.

The Sowing of the Seed

Read Mark 6:34–44. Read slowly as if you were strolling through a wheat field.

Resting in the Soil

Let these few words nurture your good soil.

> *In the oven of your heart*
> *kneaded by your love,*
> *I am blessed, broken, and*
> *ready to be given.*

The Reaping

Meditate on Mark 6:34–44.

1. The opening scene in this Scripture text offers an image of tender mercy. Seeing that vast crowd, Jesus knows they are hungry for more than bread. He begins to teach them. If this moment were today and you were in that crowd, what would you want Jesus to teach you? Spend time with that question. The moment is now. You are being taught by God.

2. Can you remember a time when you wanted to send someone away rather than provide nourishment out of your own resources? Perhaps you have even tried to send a part of yourself away rather than feed it. A hungry, gifted part of you wants some of your time, your energy, your affirmation, your presence. Ignoring your soul needs is a kind of dismissal. Reflect on these things.

3. Spend time with Jesus' question, "How many loaves have you?" The loaves represent whatever in your life needs to be broken and shared with others, for example, your time, your ideas, your laughter, your stories, your listening heart, your compassion, your joys and sorrows, your presence. . . . Name your loaves.

Songline

How many loaves do you have?

The Song of the Seed

Jesus, I want your insightful question to accompany me through this day. How many loaves do you have? The question falls into the good soil of my heart, and I am led to take inventory of my loaves. How richly you have blessed me! May I always find myself willing to break these loaves with others and to be taught by you. I am in that vast crowd of Mark's Gospel feeling lonely and hungry myself. Your mercy washes over me. You love me, and I am fed. I want to do for others what you have done for me. The gifts I have received I want to give freely.

May it come to pass!

Gleanings

Today my songline followed me well. I often found myself present to the wonder of being taught by God. How important it is to be open to the grace of each moment! During one of these moments of grace, I found myself baking bread. While the bread was rising, I sat down to pray for those who have no bread, and those who have no peace. I prayed for people whose homelands have been ravaged by war and famine. I remembered, too, those who are victims of senseless acts of violence. May I always be aware of life beyond my own household.

When the bread was ready, I called in some friends to bless it. We read Mark 6:34–44. Pondering the loaves of our lives, we shared the gifts the bread symbolized for each of us. Breaking the bread, we each held a piece as we prayed the Lord's Prayer. We ate in silence, ending with a prayer.

O Jesus, Bread of Life, be our constant reminder that we are bread for the world and that we, too, are called to be blessed, broken, and given. May we be enriched by your daily blessing. May we be open to your daily breaking. May we be willing to be given as your gift of bread for the world.

CHAPTER 3

Day 3—
The Gift of Listening

Focus for the Day

Tending your prayer life even when everyone is looking for you.

The Fallow Season

Soak up the quiet for a few moments. Be absorbed in God.

The Sowing of the Seed

Read Mark 1:32–39 . . . slowly.

Resting in the Soil

Let this simple message usher you into the Great Mystery.

> *Into a holy darkness*
> *quietly I move,*
> *Soaking up the stillness*
> *absorbed in God.*

The Reaping

Meditate on Mark 1:32–39.

1. One line from our reading for today could be a bit overwhelming, "And the whole city was gathered around the door." When everything and everyone seem to be crowding in on you, it may be time for some healthy self-maintenance. Listening to your own weariness can enable you to be a better listener to those knocking at your door. How do you feed your soul? Where do you go for renewal? Give yourself the gift of listening to your deepest need today.

2. Imagine that you are in the crowd outside Jesus' door. Your own anxieties are making it difficult for you to listen to the pain of others. Name some of your anxieties. Choose a specific area of tension for your main focus as you stand outside Jesus' door with the crowd. Listen to this anxiety of yours. Ask Jesus to listen with you.

3. Ministering to others does not mean killing yourself. Even if everyone is looking for you today, listen to Jesus calling you to care for your soul. "Listen, or your tongue will keep you deaf."

Songline

Listen, or your tongue will keep you deaf.

The Song of the Seed

O Sower of the seed, I long to be absorbed in you, caught up and held in a plan that's bigger than my own. If I am absorbed in you, no longer will you be a hidden God, for I will be hidden in you. Then when everyone is looking for us, they will find you in me and I in you. Jesus, if I can be a blessing to one person today—

and if I can receive a blessing from someone—I will know that I have lived this day with a listening heart. O Sower of the seed, plant me in the heart of the world absorbed in you.

May it come to pass!

If possible, use Michael Card's song "Will You Not Listen?" for your prayer today.

Gleanings

The day star is gone. The night lights have come. I sit by my window in candlelight and process my day. Keeping company with my prayerful heart today, I listened to some of the problems, anxieties, and fears I've been avoiding. Making a specific effort to live this day absorbed in prayerful listening has made me more aware of how God listens to me. Through this mutual listening, my capacity for God increases, and I am transformed. The transformation may be ever so small, and the people I live with may not even notice it. But I notice it! Tonight I can hold more of God. I am filled with care for someone I thought I couldn't love. She has been in the crowd at my door, and I've never really listened to her. I was trying to listen alone. Listening with the Holy One makes all the difference in the world. As I glean through this day's memories, I feel joy in having lived one day absorbed in God. I pray that when I awake Our listening will continue.

CHAPTER 4

Day 4—
The Gift of
Hope at the Tomb

Focus for the Day

Tending your Christ life!

The Fallow Season

It is soul-resting time. Practice deep breathing.

The Sowing of the Seed

Read Luke 24:1–12.

Resting in the Soil

Let these words prepare you to abide in God.

> *Taking the Word*
> *to the tomb of my heart*
> *I let go of my plans*
> *and wait for God's anointing.*

The Reaping

Meditate on Luke 24:1–12.

1. Christ's anointing power is within you. You can anoint with oils, with water, with incense, with prayer. You can anoint with words: kind words; challenging words; affirming, hopeful, loving, and compassionate words. You can anoint with your presence. All of these are ways of nurturing the Christ life in you. By tending your Christ life and sharing it with others, you bring hope to many who still stand at the tomb looking for Jesus. Reflect on these things.

2. These words "returning from the tomb, they told all" anointed me during my second reading. Most of us have experienced a sojourn at the tomb. We come looking for life and find only death. In the loneliness of our tomb-moments, it appears there is nothing left to anoint. The tomb, however, always teaches us something. The tomb taught the women that they needed to go elsewhere with their spices and perfumes. It taught them the urgency of going forth to tell their truth. Reflect on your recent moments at the tomb. What are they teaching you?

3. You come forth from your tomb with the gospel of your life. You come with news you didn't know you possessed. Sometimes the good news is new information about yourself. You come away from the tomb with gifts for anointing. You come with newly discovered ways of sharing your life. Your personal rising from the tomb is part of the resurrection story. How will you anoint your family, your church, your world? In what small way can you help others live more fully? How can the good news of your life, in Christ, help some anonymous Peter find hope again?

Songline

Anoint me with hope at the tomb.

The Song of the Seed

O Christ, Anointed One of God, each time you find me in turmoil at the tomb, you breathe into my dried-up heart new hope. Yes, even at the tomb you speak of life.

I want to be among those whose days are spent enhancing life. I want to bless and affirm every hint of life, no matter how small the glimmer may be. Kindle in me a desire to heal broken hearts. Teach me to anoint with the sacramental presence of my life. Encourage me to look for signs of life at every tomb. May I never be afraid to learn about life in the midst of death. Even at the tomb I want to celebrate the gift of hope.

May it come to pass!

Gleanings

I spent time at my tombs today. The tomb of patriarchy took much of my time. I sat there with my jar of ointment wondering what to anoint. How does one anoint that which seems so stale and idolatrous? Then I heard the angel at the tomb saying, "The anointing is already happening." Even at this *tomb there is hope, for she is rising. She is out there already bearing her alabaster jar of hope. She is shaking off the old names and claiming names of her own. She is uttering truths long stored away. She is claiming her holiness. She is breaking the silence of the ages. She is kneading the bread of tomorrow. She is listening to life. She knows that life is elusive at times, hidden in unnoticed buds, hidden in the soil's deep earth, hidden in hearts that could be on fire, hidden in patriarchy. She sees what those who choose to stay in their discouragement cannot see. She sees the love that waits for that which is patriarchal in us all to hand over our fear. She is rising, and she is good.*

She is bringing hope to all the tombs of the world. She makes tender what is hardened; she strengthens what is weak.

She is the feminine that has been suppressed far too long. She is Jesus. She is the Father and the Mother. She is the Brother and the Sister. Do not be afraid of her. She is our hope. And she is rising.

I turn off the light. I stand at my window. Silently I look out at the night sky ablaze with stars. I smile into the holy darkness and I pray: "I am returning from the tomb full of hope; for she is rising."

CHAPTER 5

Day 5—
The Gift of Commitment

Focus for the Day

Tending your faithfulness. Water the seed of your devotion, and your gift of commitment will blossom.

The Fallow Season

Abide in your good soil with quiet eyes.

The Sowing of the Seed

Read Matthew 19:16–22.

Resting in the Soil

Let these words guide you to the place where God waits.

> *Yearning for eternal life,*
> *I give away words*
> *that I may be fed*
> *with the Great Word.*

The Reaping

Meditate on Matthew 19:16–22.

1. Eternal life is in your heart. This is one of the truths the angel whispered in your ear at birth. What are the things that keep you distanced from your memory of that eternal life?

2. Reflect on your faithfulness to the commandments listed in this text. Examine each one with a contemplative heart.

3. Let the seeker's words from our Gospel story echo in your own heart: "Teacher, I have kept all these. What do I still lack?" Perhaps the answer to this question can be found in this spiritual letter from the early twentieth century:

> I charge you to release yourselves from the last strain of materialism for then only are you protected; I charge you to be forgiving and patient with all persons whether they be stupid, melancholy or evil and to keep your faces always uplifted to the highest intent, for this, above all, releases your life from all violence; I charge you to live in faith, for this will give you a splendor, a light which will be manifest to all the bewildered, the lonely, the harassed—a beacon in the storm. Stand to your full stature, for I bear witness that eternal love can be reached.[5]

Songline

Teacher, what must I do to possess everlasting life?

The Song of the Seed

Jesus, of all the gospel seeds that have ever fallen into the soil of my life, this is the one that refuses to leave. The song of this seed quietly, passionately challenges me. It is a haunting, stirring song of yearning. It sings of ways I can learn how to be more faithful to this seed planted in my soul. Thank you for keeping the song alive. Teacher, I am still longing for eternal life. I long for the gift of commitment.

May it come to pass!

Gleanings

I chose to spend this day in a desert solitude. I went with a consuming desire to surrender to this persistent seed. I took nothing with me. No books! No writing materials! No lunch! I was unable to go without thoughts, so I nurtured my thoughts that they would be peaceful. I walked a lot. In fact, it turned out to be a kind of spiritual walkabout.* A long, loving gaze accompanied me on my walk. I looked contemplatively upon everything along the way. My songline, "Teacher, what must I do to possess everlasting life," settled into the rhythm of my walking.

This evening as I glean the fields of my heart, I hear again what I believe to be the answer to my Songline: "I charge you to release yourself from the last strain of materialism for then only are you protected." Pondering these words, I remember the thoughts and opinions, the possessions and props, the schedules and agendas that keep crowding out the original purity of my life. Again I am reminded of Jesus saying, "If you have kept all these commandments then leave everything and follow me." A poem from Rumi stirs in my heart:

> I can break off from anyone,
> except that presence within.
>
> Anyone can bring gifts.
> Give me someone who takes away.[6]

---

* *Walkabout* is a term used by the Australian aborigines to denote a ritual journey for the purpose of communing with their ancestors. It could, perhaps, be akin to the Native Americans' *vision quest.*

This "presence within" has been so abiding and so patient with my fear of commitment. Jesus keeps offering me the gospel that won't go away. He longs to take from me anything that might endanger the pure gift of my free spirit.

I have allowed so much in my culture to smother that beautiful aboriginal spirit that I had in the beginning. I must regain the courage to continue my wilderness walkabout. I will go into the desert of my heart and find my true self. To go on this gospel journey, I will need to stop clinging to the safety of what I know. Again a poem from Rumi ministers to my hesitant heart:

> I pretended to leap
> to see if I could live *there.*
>
> Someday I must actually arrive there,
> or nothing will be left to arrive.[7]

CHAPTER 6

Day 6—
The Gift of
the Light of Life

Focus for the Day

Tending the light within.

The Fallow Season

The Word of God is about to make an entrance into the sacred
darkness of your good soil. Practice deep breathing as you wait.

The Sowing of the Seed

Read John 8:12–16.

Resting in the Soil

Go where these words lead you.

> I know where I came from
> and where I am going.
> I hold the Word in my heart
> until it holds me.

The Reaping

Meditate on John 8:12–16.

1. Spend some time immersed in this promise of Jesus: *If you follow me, you will have within you the light of life.* This borrowed light is your gift to share with the world. Keep it burning. How will you attend the flame today?

2. Meditate on the truth that you, like Jesus, have come from God and are going to God. You, too, have at your side the One who called you. The One who sent you will accompany you.

3. It is easy to judge by appearance. Pray for anyone that you, in your human weakness, may have judged rather than loved.

Songline

I possess the Light of Life.

The Song of the Seed

Jesus, God of Light and Life, it is you I possess when I possess the Light of Life. I was born from the circle of your light, and so I, too, can say, "I know where I came from; I know where I am going." I am a spark from the Great Light. I am returning to the Great Light. I, too, shine in the darkness. I am your disciple. I carry within me the Light of your Life. Today may this Light shine on those I have judged. I want my judging to be changed into loving.

May it come to pass!

Gleanings

As I romanced the Word today, I felt challenged and comforted. I became present to people I have judged in the past. I know that if I am truly bearing the light of life, people ought to feel as safe with me as they are with Jesus. This has not always been the case. How crucial it is for me to be the presence of Christ wherever I am!

When I insist on having complete control of my life, I block light. I create my own kind of darkness, and for a few moments, at least, I follow not Jesus but my own will. At moments like these, I forget where I came from and where I'm going. Finally, with God's grace I am able to return to the place where the light is. In this knowing place I always find restoration and peace. Attending the light within, I am able to give the light again.

I close this day by praying again for those I have judged rather than loved. I picture each person surrounded by the Light of Christ. For each person individually, I pray,

> *May there always be a little light in your darkness.*
> *May there always be a little faith in your doubt.*
> *May there always be a little joy in your sorrow.*
> *May there always be a little life in your dying.*
> *May there always be a little hope in your despair.*
> *May there always be a little courage in your fear.*
> *May there always be a little slow in your hurry.*

My words have become a blessing. I feel a softening of the heart. Blessing is so much healthier than judging.

CHAPTER 7

Day 7—
The Gift of Your Potential

Focus for the Day

Tending your spiritual wardrobe. These are the clothes you are to put on: mercy, kindness, humility, meekness, patience, forgiveness, love, peace, gratitude, wisdom, Christ.

The Fallow Season

Sit silently with the good soil of your hallowed ground. Rejoice that there is within you so much potential for growth. Practice deep breathing as you wait for the Word.

The Sowing of the Seed

Read Colossians 3:12–17. Read slowly and if possible, aloud.

Resting in the Soil

Let these few words lead you into contemplation.

Leaning back
into my good soil
I soothe my weary mind
and put on Christ.

The Reaping

Meditate on Colossians 3:12–17.

1. Consider your tremendous potential for goodness. Deep within you is a powerful seed—the stuff out of which saints are made. This is the seed of truth that wants to take root in you, the Word of God for you. Nurture that seed today.

2. The power of each virtue mentioned in your reading is already in you. Take these virtues to heart one by one with loving devotion. Call to mind a particular time when each of these virtues was alive in you. Be grateful for that memory.

3. Pray that the roots of each virtue will grow ever more deeply into your good soil. Name each virtue aloud. Prayerfully long for these virtues to be a deeper reality in your life. Longing, in itself, can be a good prayer.

Songline

May the Word of Christ find a home in me.

The Song of the Seed

May the mercy of Christ be the cloak I wear. May the kindness of Christ be my life's seasoning. May the humility of Christ be the truth of my life. May the meekness of Christ permeate my being. May the patience of Christ be at home in me. May the forgiveness of Christ flow out of my heart. May the love of Christ wrap me 'round. May the peace of Christ reign in my heart. May the gratitude of Christ be my soul's song. May the wisdom of Christ be my teacher. May the Word of Christ be my heart's true home.

May it come to pass!

Gleanings

Today I discovered that it is helpful to recite prayer sentences, songlines, as though they are true in my life, even if they aren't. I wrote down each virtue on small pieces of paper. I put them in my right pocket and went for a walk. One by one I pulled out each virtue and spent time with it. "I am filled with the mercy of God. . . ." I prayed slowly, over and over again, as I walked. Then when the time seemed right, I would put that virtue into my left pocket and draw another.

Because I have difficulty with patience, it was somewhat uncomfortable for me to say, "I am filled with the patience of God."

I found this to be a very prayerful lesson. Now as I sit in the soft shadows of my lamplight, I realize in a new way that the patience of God truly is within me. I have neglected my spiritual wardrobe too long. This evening it feels as though I have put on Christ. I have tended the good soil of my life.

CHAPTER 8

Day 8—
The Gift of
Unconditional Love

Focus for the Day

Attending your heart.

The Fallow Season

Quiet your soul, and open your heart to the One who loves you.

The Sowing of the Seed

Read Luke 6:27–38.

Resting in the Soil

Let Love lead you to your sacred center.

> *Falling into God*
> *I fall into love,*
> *for God is love*
> *I am falling in love.*

The Reaping

Meditate on Luke 6:27–38.

1. Depending on your heart's attitude, you can look at this text as a list of impossible commands or as a loving challenge. Obviously Jesus knows that a seed has been planted in that frightened heart of yours. If you tend the seed, it will break open and you will find within yourself a gospel creature utterly free to love with extravagance. Would you like to meet that gospel creature? Would you like to live in love? Go to your knowing place and wait for your instructions. Listen with the ear of your heart.

2. Who are the great lovers in the pages of your life? Name them and meditate on their lives. Draw courage from their love. Who are your enemies? Bring into the oven of your heart people you don't like very much, those you have gossiped about, those you envy, those who have hurt you. Having brought these people to your heart, pray for each one. What can you learn from each person? Do you need to forgive anyone?

3. We live in a violent world. How do you experience violence in your personal life? How are your thoughts, words, and actions poisoned with violence? Many people throughout the world are choosing to make private vows of nonviolence. This is their commitment to be peacemakers in their personal lives. Pray about this today. Gandhi once said that Christians seem to be the only ones who haven't noticed that Jesus was nonviolent. Would you consider making a vow of nonviolence? (For more information, see "Resources.")

Songline

I am in God—I am in love.

The Song of the Seed

O God of Loveliness—God of Love,
Your invitation to love is a bit overwhelming.
I feel poor in love, yet rich in longing.
Perhaps I will find the loving in the longing.
Lover of my Soul,
Make your home in the center of my being
on the throne of my heart.
Your lonely, lovely creature
longs to live in love; teach her.

May it come to pass!

Gleanings

It would take a tremendous freedom to love as described in
Luke 6:27–38. Jesus used very strong language about loving
one's enemies. Perhaps he is trying to tell me that if I want to
love I have to die a little—maybe even a lot. Is there anything
in my life that I would be willing to die for? That is a lonely
question. My eyes well up with tears as I ask it. I'm not sure I
know the answer. I remember long ago wanting so much to go
to Selma, Alabama, for the civil rights march. At that time I
thought it really wouldn't matter to me if I got killed. I like
that memory of being willing to die. But what has happened to
me today? Is there anything so important I would die for it?

Sometimes a special book acts as a catalyst for me and
challenges my tendency to live away from my heart. Sheila
Cassidy's book Good Friday People has been doing that for me
these days.[8] It is stirring up questions and insights. How easy it
is to forget the lover within. What have I lost in my living?
Reading about great lovers reminds me that I'm made out of
the same stuff they are. I spent a lot of time in my knowing

place today, and right now I feel as if I know more than I can handle.

Reflecting on the gift of unconditional love, I am remembering Maximilian Mary Kolbe. In the Nazi terror of 1941, a prisoner escaped in Poland. The commandant announced that ten men would have to die in his place. As the men were being marched to their death, Fr. Maximilian requested that he be allowed to die in place of Francis Gajowniczek, who had a wife and children.

Today I sat at the feet of those who dared to love with extravagance. They have blessed me. Their love stories may seem more dramatic than mine. But my love is a blessing, too, even when I cannot see the results. To wait to love until a big moment arrives would be a way of preventing God from being love in me. To love! No matter what! Little or big! That is unconditional love! Florida Scott-Maxwell says it well, ". . . love at any age takes everything you've got."⁹ If at this moment my love seems small, I will give what I've got.

CHAPTER 9

Day 9—
The Gift of
the Buried Treasure

Focus for the Day

Tending the treasure hidden in your field, and remembering the reign of God within you.

The Fallow Season

Begin with a few moments of centering. Practice deep breathing. Let God have you.

The Sowing of the Seed

Read Luke 12:32–34 and Matthew 13:44–46.

Resting in the Soil

Let these few words lead you to the treasure.

> *Entering the field*
> *where the treasure rests*
> *I grow rich*
> *just by sitting still.*

The Reaping

Meditate on Luke 12:32–34 and Matthew 13:44–46.

1. Imagine that the field where the treasure is buried is the field of your heart. The treasure is Christ. Your soil is the reign of God. This is the Great Mystery to which you must bow: you are the land of God. Walk through this day tending the treasure hidden in your soil. Give Jesus space to move freely in your life singing up the country of your heart. Thus, when people meet you they can truly exclaim, "Here is the land of God."

2. Where your treasure is, there is your heart. List some of your treasures. Evaluate these treasures. Hold each one up against your life. Are you good for each other? Reflect seriously on how to let God be your greatest treasure. In your opinion, what would you need to let go of, "sell," for this to be a reality in your life?

Songline

I am the land of God.

The Song of the Seed

O Treasured One, long have you hidden in the ground of my being. Truly, I can proclaim, "I am the land of God." Yet as the days wear into months, it is easy for me to forget my hallowed ground and let the gift that you are remain hidden. Today I will sing a song of encouragement to my restless heart that continues to give so much of its devotion to treasures that rust and fade. I will move through this day chanting over and over again,

> *I am the land of God.*
> *I am hallowed ground, sacred soil.*
> *I am a home for a treasure that will not rust or fade.*
> *I am the land of God.*

And even as I sing my song, deep within I hear your song. You are singing up the country of my heart.

May it come to pass!

Gleanings

From earliest years I have been a collector of treasures: pressed flowers and leaves, pine cones, driftwood, shells, rocks. I have filled my journal with treasured memories: people who have gifted my life, celebrations, quotes from books and movies that have fed my soul, memories of beauty. As I evaluate my treasures, I realize that most of them have nourished my life. Among my greatest treasures I list friends, nature, and my deep yearning for God.

What puzzles me tonight as I pray with these special gifts is my tendency to allow the greatest treasure to remain buried in my soul to the extent that I do. I certainly cannot say I have never felt the Divine Presence stirring in the depths of my being, or that I have never invited this treasure to the topsoil of my life. I have! Yet something is missing. I keep yearning for a Presence I already have. I often allow that Presence to remain a buried treasure.

I am beginning to recognize that certain successes in my life have been accompanied by a tendency to omit long periods of intimate dwelling in God. Perhaps success has become a kind of god that feeds my ego in unhealthy ways. I am determined to plow up my soil and unearth the one treasure in my life that will never rust or fade. At the end of this day, I stand up and bow to the Treasure within. I am the land of God; yes, the Reign of God is within me. I receive this gift anew.

CHAPTER 10

Day 10— The Gift of Communion with God

Focus for the Day

Attending the glory of God in you. Jesus shares his glory with you. Live on in that glory.

The Fallow Season

Rest for a few moments in the glory of God. Relax, and breathe deeply as you await the Word.

The Sowing of the Seed

Read John 17:17–26.

Resting in the Soil

Envision a healing through this communion with God.

> *The glory of God*
> *streams into my soul.*
> *My open wounds*
> *accept the healing rays.*

The Reaping

Meditate on John 17:17–26.

1. In meditating on these beautiful words from John's Gospel, keep in mind that Jesus is praying for each one of us, because we, too, are disciples. Jesus prays that we will be consecrated in the truth, that we will all be *one,* and that each of us will be open to receiving God's glory into our lives. What is this glory? It is the brightness of God living on in each of us. It is the Divine Presence as revealed in our lives.

2. Review this prayer of Jesus. "I pray not only for these but also for those who through their teaching will come to believe in me. . . . I have given them the glory you gave to me, that they may be one as we are one." If Jesus prayed for you once, he will pray again. Ask him to pray for you now. Trust that he knows what you need. Be absorbed in Jesus' prayer for you. You may find yourself wondering what he prayed for. Listen with the ear of your heart. It may be revealed to you.

Songline

Live on in me.

The Song of the Seed

Having asked Jesus to pray for you, let this prayer continue as you go on a spiritual walkabout. Go with empty hands and open heart. Take nothing with you but the glory of God that Jesus has chosen to share with you. Walk in silence. Walk in communion with the One who is praying for you.

Gleanings

Jesus' request that I be consecrated in the truth rings through me with magnetic force. It lingers like the afterglow of a sunset. Asking Jesus to pray for me has been a very moving experience. As I romanced this Word of God today, I was touched by how much emotion Jesus displays in this text. His intense longing to share the glory he has received with us is striking. There is great depth of feeling in his prayer.

Throughout this day I attended those four beautiful words, live on in me. *These words also put me in communion with my parents and all the beloved ones of my life who have died. I called out to them, "Live on in me." I remembered those who died heroic deaths in their stand for justice. To them I cried out, "Live on in me." I believe that the glory of their lives, even now, can energize and heal me in my efforts to live as Christ in the world today.*

This has been a quiet and prayerful day of basking in the glory of God. And now at the close of this day all the night stars seem to be singing, "Live on in me."

CHAPTER 11

Tending the Mystery Within

The Gift of the Indwelling Presence

You have entered into the sacred space of your knowing place each day over the past weeks. You have tended your gifts well. As you daily nurture your gifts, you become more and more a gift to be given. It is time once again to meet with your retreat group. In this last session you will be celebrating the Gift of the Indwelling Presence. This will also be a time for encouraging one another not to be afraid to be the priestly people that you are.

1. Before coming to the group prayer session, spend time reflecting on the following Scripture passages in relation to your personal life: 1 Peter 2:9 and Matthew 5:14.

2. Read through the Prayer Service on the following pages. Throughout this week reflect on the light of Christ in you.

3. Look upon each member of your retreat group as an icon of Christ, and pray for each person by name. As the image of each person comes into your mind's eye, gaze upon that image and pray this prayer:

> May you be filled with light.
> May the Indwelling Presence of Christ heal you.

> *May your fear be changed into love.*
> *May you be a gift ready to be given.*

4. The leader will make sure the items in the following list are available. (See also "Resources.")

    a. A table with Bible enthroned

    b. A large candle

    c. Small taper candles for each participant

    d. A tape or compact disc player

    e. A recording of the song "Surely the Presence of the Lord Is in This Place"

    f. A recording of and/or song sheets for "Be Not Afraid"

Group Service

Your *sacred space* includes a table with Bible enthroned, a large lighted candle, and small unlit taper candles.

This session begins with a period of contemplative sitting. The leader calls the group to prayer by reading very slowly the opening reflection, gradually leading into the *prayer of quiet.*

A time frame of ten to fifteen minutes is suggested.

Opening Reflection

Leader: Bending! Mending! Tending!

The dance! The feast! The gift!

Each of these movements has been like a musical note in the song of the seed. During this last session, we turn our gaze once again to the gentle power resting in the seeds that were sown in our hearts throughout this retreat.

The Gift of the Indwelling Presence is the Light of your life. It is a fire that must be tended every day. It is the glory of God in you. What kindling will you use to keep the fire

burning now that your retreat is over? How will you blow upon the coals of your life each morning to rekindle the flame? (Brief pause. Then continue.)

Try to become very quiet inside.

Put your feet flat on the floor if possible.

Sit erect.

Relax your muscles.

Let your tensions go.

Close your eyes and smile gently, for smiling has a healing effect during the prayer of quiet.

Breathe deeply, in and out, in and out, in and out . . .

Be silent now as the group moves into a period of contemplative sitting. To bring the group back to attention, the leader begins praying the Lord's Prayer very slowly and then asks participants to look upon one another with love as the song "Surely the Presence of the Lord Is in This Place" is played.

Opening Prayer

> **All:** O Great Light of the Universe, as we gather for prayer, we acknowledge your glory within us. The Gift of your Indwelling Presence has become an ointment for the darkness in our lives. Each of us is a little spark from the Great Light. Thank you for sharing your glory with us. We long for the Light within us to bring hope and healing to our world. In the name of Jesus we pray,

May it come to pass!

Readings

First reading: 1 Peter 2:9.
(Brief pause.)

Gospel reading: Matthew 5:14.

Faith Sharing

("Guidelines for Faith Sharing," see the introduction)

How has the experience of praying the song of the seed enriched your prayer life? What are your plans for keeping the song alive? What insights and discoveries, struggles, dreams, or visions would you like to share with those gathered here? How can you encourage one another to believe in the Gift of the Indwelling Presence? Share briefly how each person in your group has been a light for you.

Bring faith sharing to a close by giving each person a candle. Invite participants to light their candles from the central Christ candle. All stand in a circle for closing prayer.

Be open to looking at one another. This prayer is especially effective when done at night because of the candlelight. Turn out all bright lights.

A Litany of Splendor

Leader: We celebrate the Spark of God in us. We honor the Indwelling Presence. We encourage one another not to be afraid to be who we are: the Light of Christ in our world. We look around this room and see the glory of God shining in every face. Do you know the person standing at your side? Another Christ is beside you.

All: Be not afraid to be who you are!*

Leader: My sisters (and/or brothers). Look all around

---

* *Option:* You may wish to sing the refrain from "Be Not Afraid" as a response during the Litany of Splendor rather than using the response given.

you. Do you know the person standing by your side? Who are these who have gathered here for prayer? The person next to you is God's work of art: a *beloved* one of God, chosen before the world began to be holy and full of love! Angels walk before her, before him. Joyfully they sing out: "Here is God's temple on earth!" The person beside you is rooted in Christ and growing ever more deeply into Christ. In the heart of the one beside you dwells the ever-living God. Look around you and be in awe. Don't be afraid!

All: Be not afraid to be who you are!

Leader: The person next to you is a seed that must fall into the ground and die in order to know the fullness of life. There is a life here that must be lost in order to be found. The person beside you has a journey to make. It is not an easy journey. It is a journey to Jerusalem. The steps along the way are often painful, yet in the heart of the one beside you is a tremendous resilience, an inner strength that comes from God. The person beside you can bear incredible hardships. Within that person is an ocean of life. She or he is strong, loving, wise. With your encouragement this inner strength can be discovered and lived a little more each day. So don't be afraid.

All: Be not afraid to be who you are!

Leader: The person next to you is a light for the world— a light, a flame, a star. The person beside you is salt for the earth. The earth is made better by her presence, by his presence. There at your side is a treasure, a treasure in an earthen vessel: little and great, frail and glorious, poor and rich. The person next to you is broken in some way and at times finds that overwhelming—and yet, in the midst of that brokenness is abundant life, the abundant life that Jesus promised, so don't be afraid!

All: Be not afraid to be who you are!

Leader: The person beside you has a name, a name that must be lived out and proclaimed at the Table of Daily Life. It is the name God called out so long ago, "Do not be afraid. I have called you by name. When you pass through the waters, I will be with you." The person next to you is precious and glorious and loved deeply by God. Look around you my sisters (and/or brothers). Another Christ is beside you, so don't be afraid.

All: Be not afraid to be who you are!

Closing Song

"Be Not Afraid."
Conclude with refreshments and friendship.

Resources

Recordings of most of the songs suggested for your prayer can be found on cassette tape or compact disc. Many of these can be purchased at music stores that stock religious music. In the lists that follow, when possible I have included an address in case you need to go directly to the recording company. Some of the folk songs I've suggested have been recorded by various groups, so you may know of sources other than the ones I've listed.

If you belong to a church that has a resource library, you may find what you are looking for there. If not, you may want to recommend that it be purchased. Some public libraries also lend recorded music.

Check with friends, churches, or music stores to find words and music for the songs listed.

When instrumental music is called for, use something of your own choice. A favorite of mine is *The Edge of Forever,* by the harpist Hilary Stagg, The Real Music, 1993.

Bending: The Dance

"Simple Gifts"

New England Hymns, instrumental version
MCMXC New Spring Publishing,
Division of Brentwood Music, Inc.
316 Southgate Court, Brentwood, TN 37027

Bright Morning Star Arisin', a lovely vocal folk version
Flying Fish Records
1304 West Schubert, Chicago, IL 60614

Full Body Blessing: Praying with Movement
J. Michael Sparough, S.J., and Bobby Fisher
St. Anthony Messenger Press
1615 Republic Street, Cincinnati, OH 45210

Full Body Blessing is a set of two cassettes that contain marvelous suggestions for praying with movement. "Simple Gifts" is included along with instructions for dance steps. I highly recommend this set. However, rather than spending a lot of time trying to learn the steps given on this tape, you may prefer to use free-form dancing and create your own movements. In this set you will also find a wonderful movement for "The Sower and the Seed."

"Lord of the Dance"
Even the Sparrow
New Dawn Music
P.O. Box 13248, Portland, OR 97213

Mending: The Feast

"I Will Bring You Home"
The Word (Michael Card)
The Sparrow Corporation
P.O. Box 5010, Brentwood, TN 37024

"Safety Harbor"
Safety Harbor (Rory Cooney, Gary Daigle, Theresa Donohoo)
Gia Publications, Inc.
7404 South Mason Avenue, Chicago, IL 60638

"Holy Darkness"
Lover of Us All (Dan Schutte)
New Dawn Music
P.O. Box 13248, Portland, OR 97213

"How Can I Keep from Singing?"
The Best of Struggles, Womancenter at Plainville
76 Everett Skinner Road, Plainville, MA 02762

Tending: The Gift

"Will You Not Listen?"
The Word (Michael Card)
The Sparrow Corporation
P.O. Box 5010, Brentwood, TN 37024

For information about the vow of nonviolence, write
Pax Christi USA, 348 East Tenth Street, Erie, PA 16503

"Surely the Presence of the Lord Is in This Place"
Soundtraks, Christian World, Inc.
Oklahoma City, OK

"Be Not Afraid"
Earthen Vessels
New Dawn Music
P.O. Box 13248, Portland, OR 97213

Notes

Introduction

1. William Wordsworth, "Intimations of Immortality," *The Norton Anthology of Poetry* (New York: W. W. Norton & Company, 1970), 580.
2. Meyer Friedman, M.D., and Diane Ulmer, R.N., M.S., *Treating Type-A Behavior and Your Heart* (New York: Alfred A. Knopf, 1984), 31.
3. Bruce Chatwin, *The Songlines* (New York: Viking, 1987), 14.
4. Willa Cather, *My Antonia* (Boston: Houghton Mifflin, 1918), 7.

The Groundwork

1. Marge Piercy, "The Common Living Dirt," from *Stone, Paper, Knife.* (New York: Alfred A. Knopf, 1983), 123–124.
2. Rabindranath Tagore, *Gitanjali* (New York: Macmillan, 1971), no. 3, p. 25.
3. The concept of God's ruling the world from the throne of our hearts comes from Julian of Norwich.
4. Willa Cather, *O Pioneers!* (Boston: Houghton Mifflin, 1913), 116.
5. *The Life of Teresa of Jesus* (Garden City, NY: Doubleday Image Books, 1960), 128.

Part I. Bending: The Dance

1. This story by Reverend Eido Tai Shimano is quoted in *A Listening Heart,* by David Steindl-Rast (New York: Crossroad, 1983), 83.
2. Joyce Rupp, *May I Have This Dance?* (Notre Dame, IN: Ave Maria Press, 1992), 11–12.
3. Kuki Gallmann, *I Dreamed of Africa* (New York: Viking, 1991).
4. Edward Farrell, *Free to Be Nothing* (Collegeville, MN: The Liturgical Press, 1989), 49.

Part II. Mending: The Feast

1. Charles Dickens, *Nicholas Nickleby* (New York: Thomas Y. Crowell), 176.
2. Florida Scott-Maxwell, *The Measure of My Days* (New York: Penguin Books, 1968), 28.
3. Sandra Cisneros, *Woman Hollering Creek* (New York: Random House, 1991), 6.
4. *Letters of the Scattered Brotherhood,* edited by Mary Strong (New York: Harper & Row, 1948), 171.

Part III. Tending: The Gift

1. Linda Schierse Leonard, *Witness to the Fire,* (Boston: Shambhala, 1989), 348–349.
2. *The Philokalia,* vol. 1, translated by G. E. H. Palmer, Philip Sherrard, and Kallistos Ware (London: Faber & Faber, 1979).
3. Marge Piercy, *Stone, Paper, Knife,* 124.
4. William Johnston, *Letters to Contemplatives* (Maryknoll, NY: Orbis Books, 1991), 47.
5. *Letters of the Scattered Brotherhood,* 70.
6. John Moyne and Coleman Barks, *Quatrains of Rumi: Unseen Rain* (Putney, VT: Threshold Books, 1986), 14.

7. Ibid., 6.
8. Sheila Cassidy, *Good Friday People* (Maryknoll, NY: Orbis Books, 1991).
9. Florida Scott-Maxwell, *The Measure of My Days*, 15.

Macrina's Choice:
A Bibliography

Books on lectio divina and contemplative union—biblical and monastic spirituality—and the spirituality of daily life, which is, of course, the integration of our stories with God's story.

Cassidy, Sheila. *Prayer for Pilgrims: A Book about Prayer for Ordinary People.* New York: Crossroad, 1982.

Chittister, Joan. *Wisdom Distilled from the Daily: Living the Rule of St. Benedict Today.* San Francisco: Harper & Row, 1990.

De Mello, Anthony. *The Way to Love.* New York: Doubleday, 1991.

de Waal, Esther. *Living with Contradiction: Reflections on the Rule of St. Benedict.* San Francisco: Harper & Row, 1989.

Dumm, Demetrius. *Flowers in the Desert: A Spirituality of the Bible.* New York: Paulist Press, 1987.

Easwaran, Eknath. *Take Your Time: Finding Balance in a Hurried World.* Tomales, CA: Nilgiri Press, 1994.

Finley, James. *The Awakening Call: Fostering Intimacy with God.* Notre Dame, IN: Ave Maria Press, 1984.

Hall, Thelma. *Too Deep for Words: Rediscovering Lectio Divina.* New York: Paulist Press, 1988.

Howe, Jean-Marie. *Spiritual Journey: The Monastic Way.* Petersham, MA: St. Bede's Publications, 1989.

Jager, Willigis. *The Way to Contemplation: Encountering God Today.* New York: Paulist Press, 1987.

Keating, Thomas. *Intimacy with God.* New York: Crossroad, 1994.

Livingston, Patricia. *Lessons of the Heart: Celebrating the Rhythms of Life.* Notre Dame, IN: Ave Maria, 1992.

Merton, Thomas. *New Seeds of Contemplation.* New York: New Directions, 1962.

Pherigo, Lindsey. *The Great Physician—Luke: The Healing Stories.* Nashville: Abingdon Press, 1983.

Rohr, Richard. *Simplicity: The Art of Living.* New York: Crossroad, 1991.

Rupp, Joyce. *May I Have This Dance?* Notre Dame, IN: Ave Maria, 1992.

Shannon, William. *Seeking the Face of God.* New York: Crossroad, 1988.

———. *Silence on Fire: The Prayer of Awareness.* New York: Crossroad, 1991.

Smith, Pamela. *Woman Story: Biblical Models for Our Time.* Mystic, CT: Twenty-Third Publications, 1992.

Vanier, Jean. *Community and Growth.* New York: Paulist Press, 1979.

Vest, Norvene. *Bible Reading for Spiritual Growth.* San Francisco: Harper San Francisco, 1993.

Books that will stretch your mind and heart—outstanding challenges to radical gospel living. As you read these, reflect on this question: If you were arrested for being a Christian today, would they find enough evidence to convict you?

Cassidy, Sheila. *Audacity to Believe.* Cleveland: Collins World Publishing, 1977.

———. *Good Friday People.* Maryknoll, NY: Orbis Books, 1991.

Kavanaugh, John Francis. *Following Christ in a Consumer Society: The Spirituality of Cultural Resistance.* Maryknoll, NY: Orbis

Books, 1982.

Romero, Oscar. *The Violence of Love: The Pastoral Wisdom of Archbishop Romero.* Compiled and translated by James Brockman, S.J. San Francisco: Harper & Row, 1988.

Wallis, Jim. *Agenda for Biblical People.* San Francisco: Harper & Row, 1976.

Books that acquaint you with the wisdom of indigenous peoples as well as the spirituality of those who work for their cause.

Bell, Diane. *Daughters of the Dreaming.* Minneapolis: University of Minnesota Press, 1993.

Courtenay, Bryce. *The Power of One* (a spellbinding novel of personal courage—set in South Africa). New York: Random House, 1989.

Davidson, Robyn. *Tracks.* New York: Pantheon Books, 1980.

Morgan, Marlo. *Mutant Message Down Under.* New York: Harper-Collins, 1994.

van der Post, Laurens. *A Story Like the Wind* (an epic novel of contemporary southern Africa). New York: Morrow, 1972.

———. *A Far-off Place* (sequel). New York: Morrow, 1974.

Wise Women of the Dreamtime: Aboriginal Tales of the Ancestral Powers. Collected by K. Langloh Parker. Edited with commentary by Johanna Lambert. Rochester, VT: Inner Traditions International, 1993.

Wood, Barbara. *The Dreaming: A Novel of Australia.* New York: Avon Books, 1991.

Books that will assist you in harmonizing Western and Eastern ways of prayer, enabling you to see how these two spiritual paths are needed for us to find unity and wholeness.

Aitken, Robert, and David Steindl-Rast. *The Ground We Share: Everyday Practice, Buddhist and Christian.* Conversations edited by Nelson Foster. Liguori, MO: Triumph Books, 1994.

Bruteau, Beatrice. *What We Can Learn from the East.* New York: Crossroad, 1995.

Griffith, Bede. *Return to the Center.* Springfield, IL: Templegate, 1977.

———. *The Marriage of East and West.* Springfield, IL: Templegate, 1982.

Healy, Kathleen. *Entering the Cave of the Heart.* New York: Paulist Press, 1986.

Johnston, William. *Lord, Teach Us to Pray.* London: Fount, 1990.